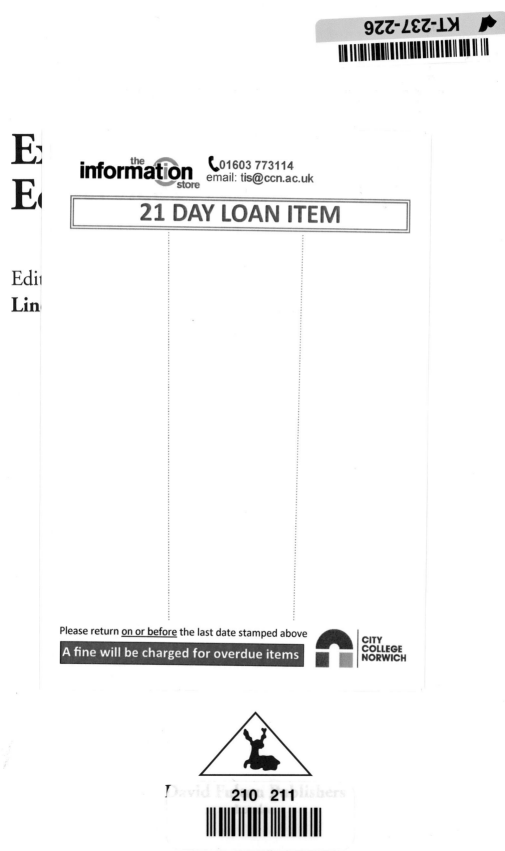

David Fulton Publishers Ltd
The Chiswick Centre, 414 Chiswick High Road, London W4 5TF
www.fultonpublishers.co.uk

British Library Cataloguing in Publication Data
A catalogue record for this book is available from the British Library.

ISBN 1 85346 848 7

Typeset by Servis Filmsetting Ltd, Manchester
Printed and bound in Great Britain.

Contents

Foreword   v
Notes on the contributors   vii
Acknowledgements   x

Part I   Exploring curriculum issues

1. Exploring issues in early years education and care   2
   Linda Miller, Rose Drury and Robin Campbell

2. Literacy in early childhood settings in two countries: a comparison of
   policy into practice issues   8
   Linda Miller, Janet Soler, Lyn Foote and John Smith

3. Exploring key literacy learning: own name and alphabet   19
   Robin Campbell

4. The essence of history in the early years   28
   Rosie Turner-Bisset

5. Drawing as a language in the early years   40
   Rosemary Allen

6. Developing thinking skills through scientific and mathematical   52
   experiences in the early years
   Jane Devereux

7. Researching young children   62
   John Oates

Part II   Exploring issues of inclusion

8. Who's listening? Who's teaching? Good circumstances for the language
   development of young bilinguals in early years settings   78
   Tim Parke and Rose Drury

9 Parent partnership and inclusion in the early years   90
     Alice Paige-Smith

10. Including a deaf child in an early years context: issues for practitioners   101
     Joy Jarvis

11. Health inequalities in early childhood   112
     Angela Underdown

12 Work, play and learning in the lives of young children   124
     Martin Woodhead

     References   135
     Index   148

Foreword

It is fair to say that during almost the whole of the twentieth century, no government had either the conviction or the will to undertake the funding and promotion of truly appropriate education for children under 5 – the statutory school starting age. This was in spite of the ever-increasing evidence, from experts such as the authors of this book, that the learning experiences children had during these first few years of life were fundamental to their subsequent development as human beings. Moreover, the political lack of will was disconcerting to say the least. After all, every adult (even a politician) has had a childhood, and has memories of that time, and will often refer to the ways in which their future development into adulthood was powerfully affected by what happened to them in those early days; so to have ignored those insights into their own lives is an enigma, especially for those people well-versed in child development who tried to persuade the powers-that-be of their poor judgement.

Fortunately, in the late 1990s early years education was, for the first time, taken seriously, and much progress has taken place in raising the profile of these foundation years, and in enhancing the provision for them. These changes have been considerably influenced by the testimony and writings of educators like the authors of the wide-ranging topic in this book, and we must all be grateful to them for their consistent and continued work in fighting for the rights of our young children.

In the 1960s, 'child-centred' education was the 'in thing' – we should start from and with the children and their abilities and concerns, and plan our curricula around them. But, over the years, 'child' became almost a rude word, and was dropped in favour of 'learner'; thus, in my view, missing the point that the development of *all* aspects of the child should be our aim. Having said that, the majority of early years practitioners still 'start from the child', in spite of all the structured literacy and numeracy curricula that they are expected to follow. It is interesting and heartening to note, as one reads the chapters in this book, that a holistic and, dare one say, child-centred approach runs throughout, reiterating the need for developmentally appropriate approaches to teaching and learning. So whether discussing drawing as a language; science or history; special needs or parent partnership; comparative education or bilingualism; play or health; train-ing or children working; the emphasis is on, rightly in my view, an integrated approach.

The authors are all well-known experts in the field of early childhood, and what they are saying here is needed and timely. I wish the book the success it deserves.

Jenefer Joseph
Consultant in Early Childhood Education

Notes on the contributors

Rosemary Allen is Senior Lecturer in Art and Design Education at the University of Hertfordshire. She teaches on a range of courses including early years education, primary and secondary art and design, and supervises students on the CPD programme. She has wide experience of teaching in schools and as an advisory teacher for art and design. Her current interests are art and its role in the development of language and in learning styles generally.

Robin Campbell is Emeritus Professor of Primary Education at the University of Hertfordshire. He was previously a primary school teacher and head teacher. His research interest is early literacy development and his most recent books, including *Literacy from Home to School: Reading with Alice* and *Read-Alouds with Young Children*, reflect that interest.

Jane Devereux is Senior Lecturer in Education at the Open University and formerly Director of Primary Initial Teacher Education at the University of Surrey, Roehampton. Her main interests are early childhood education, children as learners and primary science. Her research and publications include observing young children, science education and professional development of practitioners and teachers.

Rose Drury is Principal Lecturer in Early Years Education at the University of Hertfordshire, where she is programme leader for the BA (Hons) Early Childhood Studies and other Early Years Education courses. She has extensive experience of teaching bilingual children in the early years. Her research and publications relate to this field.

Lyn Foote is Director of Programmes in Early Childhood Teacher Education at Dunedin College of Education, New Zealand, and has worked in teacher education in the Pacific Nations of Solomon Islands and Niue. Her research interests include home-based early childhood education and early literacy.

Joy Jarvis is Principal Lecturer at the University of Hertfordshire. Her chief responsibilities are training teachers of the deaf. She is also closely involved in early years education. She has worked with children with a range of communication difficulties in different contexts, including homes and schools and has published in this field.

Linda Miller is Lecturer in Childhood Studies at the Open University and formerly Principal Lecturer in Early Years Education at the University of Hertfordshire. She has worked both with and for children throughout her professional life. Her research and publications include the area of early literacy development, working with parents, play and the early years curriculum.

John Oates is Senior Lecturer in Psychology in the Faculty of Education and Language Studies at the Open University. He chairs the production of the Child Development course in the OU's psychology degree programme. He also chairs a research group concerned with developmental psychopathology, the area in which his main research activity is located.

Alice Paige-Smith is Associate Lecturer and consultant Research Fellow at the Open University. She was formerly a Senior Lecturer at the University of Hertfordshire. Her main work and publications are concerned with inclusive schooling.

Tim Parke is Principal Lecturer in Linguistics at the University of Hertfordshire. He has taught in most sectors of education, including higher and adult education classes. He writes mainly about bilingual children, looking at issues of literacy, language gain and loss and family language practices.

John Smith is Principal Lecturer and Head of Education at Dunedin College of Education, New Zealand. He has written extensively on literacy and has taught young children as well as tertiary students and teachers.

Janet Soler is Lecturer in the Curriculum and Teaching Centre at the Open University and was formerly a lecturer at the University of Otago, New Zealand. She has taught in primary and secondary schools in both England and New Zealand. Her recent research and publications include current, historical and comparative developments of policies and practices in literacy teaching. She has also published on ICT and web-based development for schools and higher education.

Rosie Turner-Bisset is Senior Lecturer in Primary History Education at the University of Hertfordshire. Her research interests include initial teacher education, teaching and learning, history education, and curriculum development. She regularly teaches in early years settings to develop new materials and teaching strategies. Other publications include *Expert Teaching: Knowledge and Pedagogy to Lead the Profession*.

Angela Underdown is a Senior Lecturer in Early Childhood Studies at the University of Surrey Roehampton. She has wide experience of working with and for children and families as a health visitor, a teacher of early years practitioners and as a health policy advisor at The Children's Society. Her particular interests include inequalities in child health and the importance of supporting early relationships as a foundation for positive emotional wellbeing.

Martin Woodhead is Senior Lecturer in the Centre for Childhood Development and Learning at the Open University. He has written numerous books and articles on early childhood, and on child labour. He has worked on these issues with international organisations, including the Council of Europe, Save the Children and the OECD.

Acknowledgements

The success of our previous book *Looking at Early Years Education and Care* (Drury *et al.* 2000) suggested that a second text that explored some of the issues further would be worthwhile. As before, we have brought together a number of writers. On this occasion those writers are, in the main, from the Open University and the University of Hertfordshire. Those two universities have contributed in a number of ways that enabled the book to be completed and we acknowledge that contribution. In particular, Val Faulkner at the University of Hertfordshire collated all the chapters, reminded us of inconsistencies and made other helpful suggestions as the book was being written.

PART I

Exploring curriculum issues

Exploring issues in early years education and care

Linda Miller, Rose Drury and Robin Campbell

Our book *Looking at Early Years Education and Care* (Drury *et al.* 2000) was written at a time of great change in relation to early childhood provision. That book was intended to address the implications of some of those changes for early years practitioners. Much of this change has been positive, and as we wrote at that time, young children and their families, and those adults who support them, have been put firmly on the political agenda. However, change almost always brings uncertainty and issues arise which early years practitioners need to confront and address. We have chosen to explore some of these issues in this book, sometimes taking a comparative stance in order to achieve a greater understanding of our own perspective. The book is organised into two Parts. In Part I we explore issues relating to developments in the early years curriculum and in Part II we turn to issues relating to inclusion.

Exploring curriculum

In the recent past the curriculum in many early years settings in the United Kingdom had not always been written down or planned (Edwards and Knight 1996). This practice left adults working in these settings vulnerable and open to criticism. More recently, in the mid to late 1990s, published curriculum documents covering children aged 3 to 5, were introduced in all four countries of the United Kingdom – Northern Ireland (CCEA 1999), Scotland (SCCC 1999), Wales (QCAAW 2000) and England (QCA 2000). These introduced a generic framework for practice into many early years settings and helped practitioners to plan for children's learning. This development, coupled with increased accountability through inspection systems and assessment of young children on entry to schools, has led to increased demands on the skills and knowledge of practitioners and to the recognition of the need for a new professionalism. This need has been recognised through government initiatives, which we explore in the final section of this chapter.

In England, in 2000, the introduction of a new Foundation Stage of education for children from age 3 up to age 5 i.e. to the end of reception year, was intended to offer an entitlement curriculum across a diverse range of early years provision and to provide a more appropriate curriculum for the youngest children in primary schools. However, concerns have arisen about links to the primary school curriculum and the prescriptive nature of the model, which is leading some early years settings to introduce formal learning too soon (David and Nurse 1999).

In the chapters that follow, reference is made to curriculum frameworks in other countries such as New Zealand, where curricular experiences are represented through the metaphor of a woven map incorporating links across learning areas, culture and language (Ministry of Education 1996). Within the 'emergent curriculum' of the nurseries of Reggio Emilia in Italy (Rinaldi 1995), the child is seen as having 'a hundred languages' through which he or she can communicate ideas and experiences (Malaguzzi 1996). The unwritten curriculum of these Italian nurseries is made visible through a 'pedagogy of documentation' in which the children's work is filmed, photographed, recorded and exhibited in travelling exhibitions (ibid.). This is a very different form of accountability to the external inspection process, which often accompanies curriculum frameworks and approaches in other countries (e.g. DfEE 2001).

These holistic approaches to the curriculum offer a contrast to the English Foundation Stage curriculum guidance, which if narrowly, rather than creatively interpreted, implies a linear 'stepped' model of development leading to prescribed goals. In this book we endorse the view of the Early Years Select Committee report (Select Committee on Education and Employment 2000), which supports the importance of play and exploration in promoting lasting social and educational benefits. In Part I different authors explore and describe creative ways of responding to curriculum guidance through literacy, history, creative expression such as drawing, painting and music and through scientific and mathematical experiences, which arise from children's everyday lived experiences. This creative response to curriculum guidance requires practitioners who can engage in reflective practice, enquiry and research.

Literacy is a major curriculum area for all school ages and is the subject of Chapters 2 and 3. In early years settings literacy has become a major issue in the last decade. We know that many children learn about reading and writing at both home and in early years settings that provide a print rich environment with adults supporting the children's questions and curiosity. The interest by governments in developing early years literacy curricula to reflect that success, however, may lead to quite different proposals focusing upon skill-based goals and adult direction. Educators from England and New Zealand explore the different early childhood literacy strategies in those countries in Chapter 2. They use the evidence from a comparative study to consider the impact of the two different literacy curricula on the children and on practitioners. It is a reflection of that wider debate that leads Robin Campbell to explore two predictors of reading and writing success in Chapter 3. The writing of one's own name and knowledge of the alphabet by children as they move on to school predict subsequent success. However, how that knowledge is acquired is important. Rather than direct teaching, it is argued that wider literacy provision and adult–child interactions on literacy are required.

In Chapter 4 Thomas asks 'Was this the olden days?' Time would appear to be a difficult concept for many young children. How, then, can they be encouraged to learn about history? Rosie Turner-Bisset examines some of the issues involved in teaching history to very young children. She considers the learning of young children as well as debating the most valuable teaching approaches in the early years. As she does so, links with literacy are also made apparent. In Chapter 5 Rosemary Allen examines the more familiar topic of young children's creative expression and, in particular, drawing. However, she does so with a consideration of drawing as language. She argues that children are able explore issues concerned with themselves and their world as they draw. Children extend that thinking to science and mathematics and Jane Devereux explores those topics in Chapter 6. Children's natural curiosity about their environment leads to scientific and mathematical experiences and that is enhanced when the adult is able to support the children in their explorations and thinking. Our reading of this chapter is enhanced as we follow Laura's thinking and talk about the movement of the moon. Collecting children's talk together with drawings and other artefacts as part of researching young children requires care as John Oates reminds us in Chapter 7. He explores a range of approaches that are appropriate and relevant to carrying out research with young children in early years education and care settings. What questions are important? What needs to be examined more closely? Are young children's voices heard in the process of research? Those issues and the role of young children as agents versus objects in the research process are considered.

Exploring inclusion

It is probably true to say that early years educators have always believed that they offer an open, welcoming setting for all children. However, genuine inclusion and equality of opportunity are not easy to deliver. The assumption that a common provision for all will meet all needs has to be continually challenged if educators are to respond appropriately to diversity. It is when notions of a 'norm' slip into place unnoticed that both the government's and the practitioner's intention to deliver inclusion can come to mean 'invisibility' for a child.

From the Children Act (1989) to the Race Relations (Amendment) Act (2000), there is no shortage of principled statements and statutory requirements designed to ensure that equality and inclusion are at the forefront of provision. They are principles embodied in the Sure Start initiative through its emphasis on partnership with parents and the requirement that statutory providers in health and local education authorities should work together with local communities to identify need and provide intensive support for children under 4 and their families.

Equally, inclusion is central to the *Curriculum Guidance for the Foundation Stage* which has as one of its key principles for early years education: 'No child should be excluded or disadvantaged because of ethnicity, culture or religion, home language, family background, special educational needs, disability, gender or ability' (QCA 2000: 11). It also recognises the diversity of children in early years settings and includes separate sections on 'Meeting the diverse needs of children', 'Children with special educational needs' and 'Children with English as an additional language'.

Statutory requirements and statements of principle by policy-makers need to be understood and reflected in the policies written by individual settings. However, it is only through the reflective expertise of practitioners that the intentions of the policy-makers can be implemented for individual children with their diverse experiences and needs. In a context in which national documents fail to provide detailed guidance on the practice required to meet the principles they quite properly espouse, educators need to develop strategies which match the socialisation and learning needs of individual children, including those with special educational needs or whose home language is not English, for example.

In the following chapters, the importance of investigating practice from the perspective of the child, the family and the community is highlighted. The stories of Jessica and Maria, for example, provide valuable insights into a hearing-impaired and a bilingual child's learning, and explore implications for practitioners working towards inclusive practice.

The perspectives opened through consideration of the backgrounds and experience of such children may also raise questions about the central importance of play, an entitlement recognised in the *Curriculum Guidance for the Foundation Stage.* If the model of the curriculum embodies the notions of 'preparation for school' and 'child as future pupil', we may ask if this is consistent with adequate time for exploratory play in the lives of young children. And for children and families who do not place the same value on play as a curriculum entitlement as educators, will their expectations be identified, understood and responded to? We may question whether the notion of play is 'neutral' and equally accessible for all children. Terms such as 'play', 'learning' and 'work' may be interpreted differently depending on culture, belief and social context.

In Part II Tim Parke and Rose Drury commence in Chapter 8 by examining issues for young bilingual children. For all children there may be adjustments to be made, as the language and culture of the school differ from the language and culture of the home. How much more is that so for children entering an environment in which their mother tongue is not available? So as we read about bilingual Maria in the nursery classroom, we can see the opportunities that are provided, or lost, to explore language in rich and stimulating interactions. In Chapter 9 Alice Paige-Smith considers how some parents attempted to achieve inclusion for their children with difficulties in learning or with disabilities. We learn that a professional view of inclusion may not always be similar to a parental view. Here the voices of some parents are heard as they tell their stories about their children. The establishment of a support group by, and for, the parents is chronicled and demonstrates the efforts that may be required in some instances. Joy Jarvis examines a particular aspect of inclusive provision in Chapter 10. She looks at some of the key issues for those involved with children who have a hearing loss. What strategies should be adopted to give these children access to the language of the classroom? We read how important that question is as we note how Jessica misses out on some of the language used during a group activity. The essential nature of this language is clearly identified.

Early years practitioners will know that the children in their care come from a variety of backgrounds and there are inequalities in the health of those children. Angela Underdown makes comparisons with other countries, as well as suggesting strategies for reducing inequalities in child health in the UK. The health of minority groups features in this chapter and we hear too the views of four- and five-year-old children on health. Martin Woodhead provides an even more global perspective in the final chapter. Should work have a place in the lives of young children? His historical as well as cross-cultural exploration of early childhood work provides fascinating insights into children's current contribution and future economic activity. It explores an area often missing from discussions of early years education and care.

Professionalism and the early years practitioner

The chapters in this book illustrate some of the new demands and new challenges that practitioners working in today's early year settings are facing, which many may feel unprepared for. The need for high quality training in order to respond to this changing scenario has been recognised over the years by a number of influential reports (DES 1990; Ball 1994; Audit Commission 1996). However, the traditional low status of early childhood services, low pay and poor employment conditions have limited the growth of professionalism in this field. The vast majority of people who work with young children are either unqualified or poorly qualified and have limited opportunities for career progression (Hevey and Curtis 1996). In the last section of this chapter we look at this changing scenario and explore opportunities for early years practitioners to move towards a new professionalism.

The multi-disciplinary focus of recent government initiatives such as Sure Start (Sure Start 2001) and Early Years Development and Childcare Partnerships (DfEE 1997a) has begun to open up new career opportunities and requires professionals who have a broad range of knowledge and a high level of skills that cross professional boundaries. The multi-disciplinary training required for these new professional roles has been recognised in the growth of Early Childhood Studies (ECS) degrees (Fawcett and Calder 1998) which envisaged a new role of 'educarer' that would cross the boundaries of care and education. However, these degrees have been criticised by employers for not providing practical experience, an issue now being addressed through the development of 'practice' modules (personal communication, Calder 2002), and for not being linked to agreed national occupational outcomes (QCA 1999a). One significant step in relation to career progression was that in 1998 the Teacher Training Agency in England recognised advanced subject knowledge of early years, such as that provided by ECS degrees, as an alternative to a National Curriculum subject for those wishing to progress to Qualified Teacher Status (QTS). This development was linked to government plans for qualified early years teachers to be involved in all early years settings.

In 2000 David Blunkett, then Secretary of State for Education in England, announced the introduction of Foundation degrees. These new awards were intended to offer a nationally recognised, vocationally oriented qualification designed to enhance skills and knowledge and improve employability (DfEE 2000). This development was followed in January 2002 by the launch of an Early Years Sector-Endorsed Foundation degree by the Department for Education and Skills, which has been backed by significant resources and support for early years practitioners. This new degree offers recognition and development of work-based skills and underpinning knowledge and has been endorsed by the employment sector, thus addressing the criticisms previously aimed at ECS degrees. The Early Years Sector-Endorsed Foundation degree will lead to a new employment level to be known as 'Senior Practitioner'. While the achievement of 'Senior Practitioner' status is seen as an important career goal in its own right, the degree will also provide the basis for progressing to Qualified Teacher Status through a variety of routes. The further completion of an ordinary or honours degree will also offer other career opportunities for early years practitioners (DfEE 2001). This new development should open up progression routes that have previously been unavailable to the majority of early years practitioners and will be an important step in raising the standard of education and training within this field.

Therefore, there are many changes, developments and concerns for us to consider. The contributors have explored a number of those key issues and areas. In doing so the reader is provided with two distinct voices. There is the voice of those authors as they thoughtfully explore, argue and suggest. Then there is the voice of the child, sometimes very explicitly, as we are enabled to hear and read their thoughts and comments, but also implicitly as young children are, quite appropriately, a part of every chapter of this book. Both sets of voices tell us of the need to continue to explore early years education and care as the basis for supporting future positive developments.

CHAPTER 2

Literacy in early childhood settings in two countries: a comparison of policy into practice issues

Linda Miller, Janet Soler, Lyn Foote and John Smith

Literacy learning in early childhood

Ideas regarding how children learn about literacy have changed over time and have influenced the ways in which we view young children as learners. In the 1970s notions about 'reading readiness' prevailed. These were based on a view of the child as a passive learner who needed to be taught prerequisite knowledge and skills before they could begin to learn to read, usually when they had begun formal school (Hall 1987).

In the 1980s a contrasting view arose known as the 'emergent literacy' perspective, described as 'the reading and writing behaviours of young children before they develop into conventional literacy' (Sulzby 1990: 85). This perspective offered an alternative understanding of how young children learn about literacy prior to any formal teaching and mapped the ways in which young children learn about literacy through everyday interactions with adults. It stemmed from 'naturalistic' research focusing on young children in their own homes showing how young children construct their knowledge of literacy from everyday events involving print (e.g. Bissex 1980; Laminack, 1991). Observations by one of the authors (Miller 1996) of Katie between the ages of 2 and 5 showed that she understood that the marks we call print carry meaning. For example, she would notice the print on supermarket bags and packets and ask, 'What does that say?' She wrote shopping lists and notices using the familiar letters of her own name. She 'read' the television page in the newspaper in order to find her favourite programme, thus demonstrating knowledge of what print does, even though she couldn't read the words.

More recently literacy has been seen as a social and cultural process where relationships with significant adults are seen as particularly important. Vygotsky's (1978) views have been particularly influential in emphasising the role of the adult in assisting the child to move beyond what he or she can do and understand now with assistance, to what he or she will be able to do later unaided. Observations of children in familiar settings with familiar adults have revealed children who are competent and questioning literacy learners who co-construct knowledge alongside adults (e.g. Minns 1997; Campbell 1999). Campbell's observations of his grand-daughter Alice show how she was supported in her literacy learning by family members. In a collaborative research project with early years practitioners Anning and Edwards (1999: 166) described these child/adult interactions as 'joint involve-ment episodes'. They say, 'we became more and more convinced of the importance of adults following children's learning by careful observation as the precursor to leading children, through guided participation, towards new learning'. These changed understandings about how young children learn about literacy alongside a more able adult raise questions about the sorts of environments for literacy and lit-eracy experiences we should be offering to children in early years settings. Also, whether these new understandings are reflected in national policy and national cur-riculum guidance for early childhood.

Progress in literacy development in the early years of schooling is an increasing concern of governments across the world. In England the response of the UK government has been to develop a National Literacy Strategy and curriculum guid-ance for early childhood for children aged 3 to 5. In England the guidance is linked to the National Curriculum in primary schools; consequently the requirements of primary schools to meet national literacy targets have caused a 'downward pressure' into early years settings and have been a cause for concern. An added pressure is that inspection outcomes in early years settings are linked to funding. In contrast, the New Zealand strategy for improving standards of literacy has followed a more local-ised and individualised, rather than a national approach. Despite pressure to follow government objectives, the developers of the New Zealand early childhood curric-ulum guidance have adopted a more holistic and learner-centred framework than in England. The remainder of this chapter describes the influence of national government policies and initiatives on the literacy curriculum for early childhood in both England and New Zealand.

National literacy curricula

In England international comparisons, national assessment evidence and results from literacy initiatives were used in a legislative advocacy campaign to justify the development of the National Literacy Strategy (NLS) which has given rise to the Literacy Hour and more recently the ALS (Additional Literacy Support) and ELS (Early Literacy Support). The English Literacy Taskforce instigated a literacy hour and provided a detailed account of how teachers should implement it, for children as young as 5. The New Zealand Literacy Taskforce, on the other hand, recom-mended giving priority to specific initiatives rather than a national strategy. They recommended a nationally co-ordinated system of interventions targeted at those most in need, rather than the development of a National Literacy Strategy and the teaching of a Literacy Hour.

The English National Literacy Strategy was outlined in the *Framework for*

Teaching (DfEE 1998a) document, which followed on from the release of the Report of the English Literacy Taskforce. The framework came into operation under a quasi-statutory status in all state primary schools in England in September 1998. This document set out the teaching objectives in literacy for pupils from reception to year 6. It was this document that set out the format of a Literacy Hour as a daily period of time throughout the school, which would be dedicated to 'literacy teaching time for all pupils' (DfEE, 1998a: 8).

It has been argued that this document emphasised interactive whole class teaching from the school improvement literature, which had been espoused by influential members of the Literacy Taskforce (Mroz *et al.* 2000). The framework advocates the pedagogical approaches of whole class shared reading and writing, whole class word level work, guided group and independent reading and writing and whole class plenary. This emphasis on whole class teaching and group activities is supported by Roger Beard (1999) in his outline of the rationale underpinning the Literary Hour:

> It stresses the importance of direct teaching by the use of the whole class teaching in the first half of the literacy hour and the maintenance of direct teaching with groups, and then with the class again in the second half. It also maximises effective learning time by ensuring that there is a dedicated literacy hour each day, with further suggestions on providing additional literacy learning time during the rest of the day, including extended writing, reading to the class and independent reading. (Beard 1999: 8)

The introduction of the Literacy Hour has been followed by the introduction of the Additional Literacy Support (ALS) and Early Literacy Support (ELS). The materials, strategies and lesson plans provided in these support materials were designed to 'be delivered during the group session of the Literacy Hour by teachers and classroom assistants' for these children 'who would not otherwise receive additional support in this area' (Michael Barber, writing in the Foreword, DfEE 1999a) and mark a continued adherence to the Literacy Hour and associated whole class and group teaching methods.

In New Zealand there have been increasing concerns that NZ children are falling behind the rest of the world in their level of literacy. This belief became the centre of media attention in the late 1980s and throughout the 1990s as academics and researchers entered the debates and the claims that New Zealand was undergoing a 'literacy crisis' (Soler 1999). As in England, this concern over 'falling standards' has led to calls for more formal teaching, and an emphasis upon instruction in phonics. In response to the perceived literacy crisis and criticism of reading methods the New Zealand government set up a taskforce in 1998.

The aim of the New Zealand Literacy Taskforce was to ensure that by 2005 every child turning 9 will be able to read, write and do maths for success (Ministry of Education 1999a). This need to 'raise standards' also led to the setting up of the English Literacy Taskforce. David Blunkett, the then Shadow Secretary of State for

Education and Employment, instructed the English Taskforce 'By the end of the second term of a Labour government . . . all children leaving primary school . . . will have reached a reading age of at least eleven' (The Literacy Taskforce 1997: 2). Despite the similarity between English and New Zealand government goals in addressing 'literacy standards', the New Zealand Literacy Taskforce did not recommend the adoption of a National Literacy Strategy or the centralised, uniform top-down approach to teaching literacy that was to become established in England. The aims and content of the two Literacy Taskforce Reports were similar, however, in the way they did not specifically address the question of the nature of literacy practices in early years settings.

The early childhood curriculum guidance in England

In England these policy developments and initiatives gradually impacted upon early years settings as the early childhood curriculum became more closely linked to the primary school. Some nursery schools introduced a form of the Literacy Hour causing Whitehead (1999b: 52) to write, 'It is naïve to believe that early years settings can remain untouched by the literacy juggernaut currently rolling over all our previous literacy assumptions and practices.'

In 1999, a new Foundation Stage of education for children aged 3 to 5 was introduced. The accompanying document *Early Learning Goals* (QCA 1999b) set out goals that stated what children should be learning by the end of the first year in primary school. Many practitioners and experts felt that this document placed too much emphasis on *what* rather than *how* children should learn.

Consequently the document was revised and expanded into a guidance document with comments from wide-ranging representatives from the early childhood community (QCA 2000). Although the goals for learning remained, there was a change in emphasis to describing appropriate ways in which adults might support children to work towards the goals, rather than a focus on achieving learning outcomes. There was also a greater emphasis on play. This made the Foundation Stage curriculum guidance more acceptable to the early childhood community, but reservations remained about how the guidance would be interpreted by practitioners with different skills, knowledge and levels of training. Also, the guidance clearly reflected the government agenda. In the Foreword it states, 'It is also about developing early communication, literacy and numeracy skills that will prepare children for Key Stage 1 of the National Curriculum' and 'We have worked closely throughout with our national partners, in particular the national literacy and numeracy strategy and OFSTED' (QCA 2000).

Literacy in the early childhood curriculum in England

Language, Literacy and Communication is one of six areas of learning in the Foundation Stage curriculum guidance and encompasses 20 learning goals. Some of these are concerned with exploration, creativity and communication, such as 'Explore and experiment with sounds, words and texts' (QCA 2000: 62) and 'Use language to imagine and recreate roles and experiences' (ibid.: 58). Hence in some respects the document shares similar aims to the principles and points of view concerned with exploration and communication within the New Zealand early childhood curriculum, Te Whaariki, described later in this chapter. However, other goals relate to more formal skills such as, 'Use their phonic knowledge to write simple regular words and make phonetically plausible attempts at more complex words' (ibid.: 60) and 'Use a pencil and hold it effectively to form recognisable letters, most of which are correctly formed'. A key difference between the two documents is that in the Foundation Stage curriculum guidance, steps towards the goals are clearly described and represented as three colour bands broadly linked to age. As these goals are to be achieved by the age of 5, by the end of reception year, the 'stepping stones' follow a suggested order and imply an expectation of what children might be doing at certain ages and stages, whereas in Te Whaariki the holistic and interwoven nature of literacy development is emphasised.

In both documents the important role of the adult is stressed. In the Foundation Stage curriculum guidance, alongside the 'stepping stones ' towards the goals are descriptions of what children might be doing as they progress towards the goals and what practitioners might do to support them. Te Whaariki suggests ways in which adults can foster literacy knowledge and concepts. The danger is that practitioners in England may feel pressured to help children to achieve the more easily measured and 'visible' goals, such as children being able to form letters or recite the letters of the alphabet, as Robin Campbell debates in Chapter 3.

Issues in early childhood literacy in England

At the time of writing, the English Foundation Stage curriculum guidance has only been in place for one year, so information about its impact is sparse. Evidence from the implementation of an earlier document *Desirable Outcomes for Children's Learning* (SCAA 1996) suggests that in the hands of well-trained practitioners, who have clear understandings of how young children learn, the prescribed learning outcomes can be sensitively interpreted. However, many practitioners lacked the necessary training to translate the outcomes into appropriate practice (Browne 1998; Moriarty and Siraj-Blatchford 1998; Miller 2000). Very preliminary data from the study reported later in this chapter suggest that some practitioners view the Foundation Stage curriculum guidance as endorsing what they do, whereas for others it poses a threat to established practices and beliefs.

These tensions are highlighted in Anning and Edwards' (1999) research into the ways in which early years practitioners have differing views about the purpose and approaches to literacy in the English early childhood curriculum. They also believe that play is seen by many policy-makers as a time-wasting feature of early childhood, despite research evidence to the contrary. They argue that a 'back to basics' approach to the curriculum with a strong emphasis on literacy is 'colonising' pre-school settings and is spreading its influence into some children's homes, as parents seek to improve their children's literacy skills. Policy initiatives in primary schools, such as the National Curriculum and the National Literacy Strategy, conflict with research that suggests a 'too formal, too soon' approach to learning is damaging to young children (Mills and Mills 1998). The government's own report on the early years (EEC 2000) cites evidence from research on brain development that natural activities such as play and exploration result in lasting social and educational benefits.

Play and literacy

In Western settings, play has been seen as an important vehicle for learning in early childhood (David 1990; Bruce 1991). The child's right to play has been endorsed by the United Nations Convention (United Nations 1989). In England, in the desirable outcomes document, the word 'play' barely featured (SCAA 1996; David and Nurse 1999). Although the Foundation Stage guidance includes a section on play, the learning goals and an inspection system linked to funding have created tensions for practitioners as they have focused on supporting children to achieve literacy outcomes while trying to hold onto play as a way of learning. Subsequently, in England, there has been a danger of play being squeezed out of the early childhood curriculum. In New Zealand play is a key goal within the Exploration strand of the curriculum.

The early childhood curriculum guidance in New Zealand

Since 1996 New Zealand has had an early childhood curriculum, Te Whaariki, (Ministry of Education 1996) for all early childhood settings that receive government funding, such as kindergartens and daycare centres (the term 'early childhood setting' is used in this chapter to refer to the diverse range of settings within NZ early childhood services). As in England the curriculum is intended to provide a commonly agreed framework across a diverse range of settings and practices, but the New Zealand early childhood curriculum was the result of widespread consultations with the full range of early childhood services, as well as parents. The curriculum framework is not organised under subject-linked headings, but is presented as four broad principles around which teachers can plan and set up a range of learning experiences through which the child will grow and develop. These principles are *empowerment, holistic development, family and community* and *relationships*. These principles are divided into five strands each with goals, learning outcomes and adults' responsibilities. These form the basis for child-centred activities and experiences.

Margaret Carr and Helen May, the developers of the New Zealand early childhood curriculum Te Whaariki (Carr and May 2000), were working in similar contexts to those that shaped the English Foundation Stage Curriculum, in that they had to link it to a national curriculum. Despite this pressure, they developed a cur-

had to link it to a national curriculum. Despite this pressure, they developed a curriculum framework that took into account the views of early childhood practitioners who expressed a 'local, situated and often personal view of the early childhood curriculum' (ibid.: 53), which did not necessarily fit with government objectives. The curriculum is based on a weaving metaphor rather than a 'stepped' model of development, which embraces a vision of the bicultural New Zealand child and incorporates the links between culture, language and learning.

Literacy in the early childhood curriculum in New Zealand

The emphasis in the Te Whaariki curriculum document is on exploration and communication, therefore, literacy is not directly addressed either as a principle or as a strand. However, it is referred to within some strands. Thus, Strand 4, Communication, states in Goal 2 that children 'experience the stories and symbols of their own and other cultures' (Ministry of Education 1996: 72). Adults should 'read and tell stories, provide books and use story times to allow children to exchange and extend ideas . . . children should see adults using print and numbers for creative and meaningful activities' (ibid.: 73).

Goal 3 states that children should develop 'an understanding that symbols can be "read" by others and that thoughts, experiences and ideas can be represented through words, pictures, print, numbers, sounds, shapes, models and photographs;' and that the children should become 'familiar with print and its uses by exploring and observing the use of print activities that have meaning and purpose'(p. 78). As a way of realising these 'goals', it is suggested:

> The programme fosters the development of concepts about print, such as the knowledge that print conveys a message that can be revisited, that spoken words can be written down and read back, and that written names represent a person. The children also learn that both texts and illustrations carry the story, that print can be useful, that books can provide information, and that stories carry information. (p. 79)

Thus some similarities can be seen with the content of the Foundation Stage guidelines for communication, language and literacy, but in Te Whaariki the emphasis is on children's experiences rather than the eventual achievement of specified outcomes.

Te Whaariki did little more than document what was accepted practice in New Zealand early childhood settings. The curriculum is integrated, with all the strands woven together. Indeed, the curriculum's title 'Te Whaariki' translates as strands weaving together to make a mat. It recognised the value of informal literacy activities in developing reading and writing and how the basis of these activities is oral language. Literacy practices are seen as embedded in cultural practices of myths, legends and stories, both told and read with adults demonstrating their own engagement with literacy. The Ministry of Education (1998) has recently released *Quality in Action*, which provides additional guidance to early childhood teachers.

The role of the family and community in supporting young children's literacy development has been also been recognised. In 2000 the Ministry began a public campaign to advise parents how literacy and numeracy activities could be incorporated into daily household life. Pamphlets describing informal approaches to literacy and numeracy were delivered to homes and also distributed from early childhood centres. The pamphlets, appropriately called *Feed the Mind* were well received by parents and were reprinted several times.

Issues in early childhood literacy in New Zealand

In a recent national report the New Zealand Educational Review Office (ERO 2000) (the government body charged with the responsibility for assessing standards in the New Zealand education system), argued:

> the introduction of academic work into the early childhood curriculum yields good results on standardized tests in the short term, but may be counter productive in the long term. For example, the risk of early instruction in beginning reading skills is that the amount of drill and practice required for success at an early age will undermine children's dispositions to be readers. (ibid.: 10)

In England the Early Years Select Committee for Education and Employment (2000) report came to similar conclusions. These comments from ERO, a body not noted for holding back any criticisms of educational institutions, are noteworthy because they occur in a climate where public criticism of literacy standards and practices is increasing. It also gave official recognition to the fact that literacy learning is an important part of the New Zealand early childhood education world.

This support for informal/child-centred approaches to the teaching of literacy is endorsed by research studies. Review Office reports on individual early childhood centres suggest that, contrary to anecdotal reports from some early childhood teachers, there is no evidence of the reviewers expecting a formal, skill-based approach to literacy. The philosophy described in Te Whaariki dovetails with the New Zealand school philosophy which is child-centred and is heavily influenced by theorists such as Smith (1971). Official handbooks supplied to all New Zealand classrooms emphasise reading as a contextualised meaning-based process and do not emphasise letters and sounds.

In 1996 Wylie, Thompson and Hedricks described the effectiveness of existing informal methods of teaching literacy in early childhood education settings. The literacy competencies of 307 five-year-old children were studied, within the context of a broader study of the competences of five-year-olds. Four of the six tasks from Clay's (1985) diagnostic test were used to assess the skills and knowledge the children could demonstrate. The results showed that only a small number of children scored less than half on the tests.

Further information about the existing literacy competences of five-year-olds as they enter formal schooling can be obtained from the School Entry Assessment, which uses tasks drawn from Clay's Concepts about Print Test (1985). This is a set of standardised tasks administered to all five-year-olds on beginning school. Results from a national report (Ministry of Education, 1997–1998) drawn from 6541 children summarise the findings as 'The new entrants in this group generally have little difficulty with how reading is carried out. Most new entrants can recognize letters, a full stop, and inversion of print or pictures' (ibid.: 4).

Evidence from kindergarten teacher interviews shows that the philosophies articulated in Te Whaariki are being followed and that kindergartens are not altering their practice to a more formal approach. McLachlin-Smith and St George (2000) examined the beliefs of 12 kindergarten teachers on literacy. All teachers read stories to children in large groups, had specific literacy areas in the kindergarten, involved small groups of children in literacy activities (reading, writing in a child's own book) and established kindergarten/home links about literacy. What was not reported as happening was formal teaching with an emphasis on letters and sounds.

It is therefore argued that a holistic approach to literacy in early childhood suits NZ children best. Assessment of school entry skills at age 5 shows that the informal methods used give children a rounded approach to literacy. Rather than concentrating on a narrow approach which teaches phonemic awareness and constructs reading as decoding letters to print, the richer print environment in NZ early childhood settings, supported by the broad statements in official documents, should and must be maintained if NZ is to produce a literate society.

A meeting of the writers of this chapter in New Zealand in December 2000 revealed many shared concerns, as educators of early childhood practitioners and as researchers in the area of literacy practising in two different countries. Hence the seeds for a collaborative literacy research project were sown.

The Early Childhood Literacy Project in England and New Zealand

The Early Childhood Literacy Project in England and New Zealand is a collaborative research project between the Faculty of Education and Language Studies at the Open University, UK, and the Early Childhood Department of Dunedin College, New Zealand. It is taking a cross-cultural look at four early years settings in each of the two countries, in order to find out about the impact of the two different literacy curricula on the children and on practitioners. We interviewed practitioners to try to find out about their concerns, beliefs and attitudes towards literacy in their early childhood curriculum. We asked them about the impact of published guidance for literacy on their literacy practices. We also observed children to find out about the range and type of literacy experiences and literacy 'events' which were offered to them, and to see how they experienced literacy in their settings. The main focus of the observations was on print literacy, that is children learning about how print works. In the final part of this chapter we offer our impressions gained from a very preliminary analysis of the data from the early stages of the project. At the time of writing we can do no more than 'capture the essence of what goes on' in these particular early years settings (Whitehead 1999a: 72).

The early childhood literacy project in England[1]

The four settings in the project included a playgroup, a reception class, a nursery class attached to a primary school and a private nursery, reflecting the diverse range of early years provision in England. Practitioners' qualifications ranged from qualified teacher status with a master's degree to basic practice certificates. Most practitioners had undertaken some recent training relating to the Foundation Stage curriculum guidance. Each of the four settings shared common features in providing for literacy. For example, in all four settings there were 'fixed' literacy events such as story times, opportunities for name recognition and the completing of weather charts. There was also a high level of 'mark making' by the children, suggesting that if children are provided with the tools for developing writing skills they would use them. There were also some key differences. In the multi-lingual reception class language, literacy and communication were given high priority in response to the perceived language needs of these children. There were many literacy events initiated and directed by the adults and an emphasis on directed phonic activities, suggesting that the 'downward push' of the National Curriculum and the demands of national testing were also influencing the children's experiences of literacy. There was less opportunity for free choice activities than in the other three settings. In the nursery class, literacy was planned into the children's play and into ongoing project work and permeated the children's day. The playgroup staff expressed the belief that literacy should be offered through play, and this was evident for a large part of the day. However, the four-year-olds were also involved in completing worksheets relating to letters, shapes and numbers, which were regarded as essential preparation for school. This suggested a tension between expressed belief and what happens in practice and seemed to be a direct outcome of some of the policy changes outlined earlier in this chapter. The private nursery offered a home-like atmosphere, which was reflected in considerable book sharing between children and adults and imaginative play linked to stories. There was therefore less commonality of practice than in the NZ settings described below and clear differences in the 'literacy culture' in each setting.

The early childhood literacy project in New Zealand

The four settings included a suburban kindergarten, an inner city full day childcare centre, a full day mixed child care centre linked to an educational institution and an inner city kindergarten. A large degree of commonality of practice was observed across the settings. All settings encouraged children to participate in informal literacy activities which included reading of books, discussing stories, making up stories, writing lists, writing their name and writing thank you notes. Teachers were able to articulate their knowledge of literacy and their goals for children's literacy learning within their setting's programme. What was significant was the absence of structured literacy events. Clearly, the teachers of the children observed, are still maintaining a child-centred approach to literacy despite increasing pressure for more formal and structured literacy learning. A notable feature was the teachers' commitment to improving their own knowledge. All teachers had attended in-service courses in the last two years and most could name specific articles they had read for their own professional development. These teachers were aware of government goals for literacy in early childhood settings and had responded to these without compromising the traditional child-focused philosophy of New Zealand early childhood education.

Unlike the English experiences in this study, few variations were observed between the literacy cultures of the settings. Where there was variation, it could be attributed to the longer time the children spent in the setting each day. In such settings children are more likely to be familiar with each other and this seemed to result in sustained sociodramatic play based on literacy experiences. The summary of the observations in these four settings is that an appropriate literacy culture is well embedded within these NZ early childhood settings.

Conclusion

In this chapter we have reflected on shared developments, issues and concerns about the literacy curriculum for early childhood in two countries. In both England and New Zealand there is a belief that offering children an early start in literacy will give both economic and educational advantages. However, differences have been highlighted in the ways that the two governments have addressed common concerns about literacy. A key difference that has emerged has been the emphasis in England on the 'mechanics' of literacy addressed through national strategies, this appeared to be influencing two of the settings in the project to adopt more formal teaching approaches. The New Zealand policy framework has embraced a more holistic, localised and learner-centred approach. Preliminary data from the New Zealand early childhood settings show a commonality of approach among practitioners in interpreting curriculum guidance and in retaining informal literacy practices. In England common guidance seems open to more diverse interpretation dependent upon the 'culture' of the setting, the training and beliefs of practitioners and the age of the children. In both England and New Zealand there is recognition that all children are entitled to become literate in an increasingly competitive world. However, it is early childhood practitioners in the two countries who face the challenge of providing contexts for literacy learning that fulfil this entitlement in ways that remain playful and enjoyable.

Note

1. The authors would like to acknowledge the contribution of Dr Alice Paige-Smith for assistance with data collection and analysis for the English settings.

CHAPTER 3

Exploring key literacy learning: own name and alphabet

Robin Campbell

Introduction

There are a number of indicators that tell us that a young child is emerging as a literacy user (Hall 1987). Showing an interest in, and enjoyment of, books are often regarded as paramount (Butler 1998). After all, we know that so much literacy learning develops from engagements with books (Teale 1984). Singing and nursery rhymes, as well as playing with, and making up their own, rhymes (Chukovsky 1963) support the child's awareness of phonemes. Then, responding to environmental print (Miller 1999), and making marks that increasingly looks like writing (Schickedanz 1990) demonstrate important knowledge and understanding.

However, among the indicators there are two that have been noted in research studies (Riley 1996a, 1996b) to be clear predictors of young children's future success with reading and writing. Those are children's ability, as they enter school at five years of age, to write their own name and their knowledge of the alphabet. Furthermore, these can be observed relatively simply. It therefore comes as no surprise that among the baseline assessments of children on entry to primary school in England are 'independently writes own name spelt correctly' and 'recognises all letter shapes by names and sounds' (SCAA 1997: 3). Therefore the link between research findings and learning goals is made. If the children are able to write their own name, and they know the alphabet, they will be reading and writing well by seven years of age – the end of Key Stage 1 in England. Of course although it would seem to be useful to know whether children have achieved that learning, setting that learning as a goal may have negative influences on early years experiences.

When adults know that own name and alphabet knowledge are important literacy indicators, then that can lead to those attributes becoming part of the early years curriculum, but it can also lead to unwelcome changes in practice. For instance David *et al.* (2000) noted that 'early years practitioners in England have felt pressurised by government initiatives to include more literacy in the nursery school programme' (ibid.: 120). And more specifically 'write their own names' (QCA 2000: 64) and 'naming and sounding the letters of the alphabet' (ibid.: 60) became part of the Foundation Stage goals for children before moving on to year 1 classes at five + years of age. Goal setting puts pressure on how they are achieved.

So there appear to be tensions between some simple goals to be achieved and perhaps the use of developmentally inappropriate practices for young children. Therefore, early years staff have important questions to consider such as: What is an appropriate literacy curriculum for the early years? How will the learning goals be achieved? What are the roles of the adults in promoting literacy learning?

What is an appropriate literacy curriculum for the early years?

If we accept that being able to write one's own name and recognise the letters of the alphabet by shape and sound are important, then supporting children to work towards those goals in developmentally appropriate ways before entering school seems sensible. It is so because it will enable them to make good progress with literacy. Therefore, early years practitioners will want to help children acquire that knowledge in early years settings or in the reception year of school. However, those two features of literacy development are insufficient if that is all the child has acquired. Children need more than just the tip of the iceberg in a literacy curriculum. The children need the whole iceberg and that therefore suggests a very wide range of literacy knowledge to underpin the surface knowledge. This therefore raises issues about the content and process of the early years curriculum.

Marian Whitehead (1999a) suggested four essential strategies for literacy that could provide a broad framework for the literacy curriculum. Those were (i) talk, play and representation; (ii) rhyme, rhythm and language patterns; (iii) stories and narrative; and (iv) environmental print and messages. These are very broad areas and they encompass a wide range of literacy activities. It is not the purpose of this chapter to suggest a complete range of activities. That is covered in books elsewhere (e.g. Campbell 1996, 2002; Browne 1996). Nevertheless, there are certain key literacy activities that will be an important part of any provision that we will note here briefly.

Talk, play and representation

A starting point is talk and Corden has argued the case 'for the centrality of spoken language in the learning process' (2000: 12). Much of children's initial learning is based on talk with oneself, with other children and with adults. During that talk comments are made, questions asked, responses provided, and conversations occur. All that adds to the child's understanding. Often the talk is linked to play as young children explore their world through imaginative play and verbalise as they do so. Inevitably it seems, part of that play will include representation as the child creates a farm with bricks, with a hat becomes a fire-fighter, and creates representations of objects and people with marks that become increasingly recognisable as drawings. In time those representations begin to include letter-like marks as the child explores the world of writing.

When play corners are organised as a vet's surgery, a post office, travel agents or supermarket, literacy materials are an integral part of the provision. Hall and Abbott (1991) provide a number of examples of that kind of literacy play. Common to each is the provision by the adults of print materials such as message pads by the telephone, blank forms, writing paper and envelopes together with pencils or other writing tools; telephone directories, magazines, brochures and catalogues; possibly also a keyboard, typewriter, or simple computer.

Other opportunities for representation can be provided at a writing centre. A variety of paper and writing tools invites the children to come and write messages, cards and lists. The presence of adults to model writing and talk about writing with the children is part of the provision. All that play and time at the writing centre encourages children to write, to think about words and letters (thus learning about the alphabet), and to develop as literacy users.

Rhyme, rhythm and language patterns

Rhyme, rhythm and language patterns are found in nursery rhymes, songs, poems and many stories. Young children get great enjoyment from playing with language, and incidentally they learn much about literacy as they do so. For instance, Meek (1990) has suggested that when children have frequent opportunities to engage with and enjoy nursery rhymes and songs, they also learn and extend their phonological awareness. Children enjoy the rhythm of nursery rhymes such as:

Mary, Mary, quite contrary,
How does your garden grow?
With silver bells and cockle shells
And pretty maids all in a row.

However, here they are also developing an awareness of the '-ow' rime unit and 'gr' and 'r' onset units, even though that awareness need not be made explicit at this point. Nursery rhymes provide children with an understanding of letters and sounds although it is the enjoyment of the nursery rhyme that is reason enough to engage with this and songs and poems.

So singing nursery rhymes and songs and reciting simple poems are enjoyable as well as instructive parts of early years provision. Many practitioners use these as a means of managing the transitions to another part of the school day. However, they are an important part of the literacy provision. Although the enjoyment, and transfer of a cultural heritage, are reason enough to engage in these activities, they also teach letters and sounds (Meek 1990). The rhyme features of the poems, songs and nursery rhymes help children understand how many words are patterned. The children learn about letters and sounds and develop a solid foundation in phonological skills (Goswami 1994) – although that need not appear to be the reason.

Stories and narrative

Stories and narrative are important to young children. After all, as Bruner (1968) indicated, narrative is one way of thinking. Children and adults make sense of their world by creating a narrative of events that they experience. Children also learn from the stories that they hear told and read by adults. In many of those stories there are rhyme, repetition and rhythm. Wade (1990) refers to them as 'the three r's' of language and stories that support young children's learning. Many of the books that young children have read to them include rhyme. For instance in *Slinky Malinki* (Dodd 1990) we read about that cat:

He was cheeky and cheerful,
friendly and fun,
he'd chase after leaves
and he'd roll in the sun.

The rhyme of 'fun' and 'sun' appeals to young children and informs the children incidentally about onset and rime, as it does in nursery rhymes. It is not difficult to see how later that will help children to read and write by analogy words such as 'bun' and 'run' (Goswami 1999). Then the repetition of phrases and sentences, rather than of single words, creates a story interest for young children. And incidentally that repetition helps the children to join in as readers and become readers. In *Good-Night Owl* (Hutchins 1972) it is the repetition of 'Owl tried to sleep' that draws children into the reading and supports their literacy development. Often it is the use of rhyme and repetition that creates a rhythm to the story. For instance, in *Green Eggs and Ham* (Seuss 1960) there is substantial use of both rhyme and repetition and it appears to be those features that create a rhythm in the story. Indeed, the rhythm appears to dictate the way in which that story is read aloud to children. Of course, story does even more for young children and as Baghban (1984) and Campbell (1999) have shown, very young children comment upon how they know certain words because they saw them in particular books. So a visual memory of some words is developed, as well as much other literacy learning, as children have the opportunity to hear stories read and repeated.

So a starting point for any early years literacy activities are the daily (or more frequent) story readings or read-alouds (Campbell 2001a). We know that activity is an important one for young children and the benefits are well documented (Teale 1984). Children develop a love of books and an interest in reading, they acquire characters from stories as imaginary friends, learn words and sentences, begin to understand story structure, and appreciate the rhyme features of many books. In addition, repeated readings replicate what we know occurs at home for many children enabling them to gain ownership of the story and supporting literacy learning. Of course, for very young children the adults make the story readings interactive, encouraging the children to join in with the reading where repetitions, in particular, help that to happen. Providing opportunities for the children to respond to the stories is an important part of the activity. The children can draw, paint, make models, create puppets (which can be used during subsequent rereadings of the book), mark make and write. Thus they can represent the story in a variety of formats. As Gregory (1996) has indicated, all that can be useful also for children learning English as a second language, alongside using what those children bring to school from their own communities.

Because young children at home also are able to see the print during story readings Holdaway (1979) suggested the use of big print that all the children in the class could see. He referred to that activity as shared book experience. Subsequently known as shared reading, it has become another useful literacy activity for all the reasons we have noted in relation to story reading. However, when used as part of the literacy hour in England (DfEE 1998) it has been changed to emphasise attention to print features – looking at words, considering letters and sounds, noting punctuation and spelling patterns. The shared reading in that format is used then to teach aspects of literacy directly and there is a real danger that instead of exciting children about reading it instead diminishes an interest in books. But the shared reading can be used more appropriately for a wider purpose. As Whitehead (1999a) has argued, shared reading needs to be about the nature of literacy experience for young children. Thus it can become another form of story reading, albeit that the children now have the advantage of seeing the print, and learning about it, as well as enjoying the story.

Environmental print and messages

In our society there is a great deal of environmental print that young children will experience. Furthermore, studies of young children demonstrate that the children are curious to find out about that print. For instance, Laminack (1991) provides many examples of his young son Zachary asking questions about print as well as attempting to make sense of it for himself. Part of that questioning inevitably leads to discussions about letters of the alphabet. Currently the yellow *M* is often among the first letters to create a response from young children (e.g. Baghban 1984: 29) when they spot a McDonald's logo.

The children will experience a great deal of environmental print outside of school. However, it is particularly helpful if that print is also brought into the classroom and talked about (Miller 1999) and as Kenner (2000) demonstrated, linked to the languages of home for bilingual children. Displays of logos, creating alphabet environmental print books, having a print party with children wearing t-shirts with print, going on a print walk to look for print in the school and outside are all suggested. Then creating classroom print that is for a purpose and is talked about all adds to the children's literacy learning in a meaningful context.

Learning about letters is developed further when children have the opportunity to mark make and send messages. Initially the sending of greeting cards is an activity that children may have witnessed at Christmas, birthdays, Mother's day, Chinese New Year, etc. and enjoy replicating. For instance, Alice sent a card at 3 years 3 months (Figure 3.1), although at that stage the card included just two words 'To' and ' Gd' (Grandad) (Campbell 1999: 76)

Nevertheless, there was evidence of an involvement with the letters of the alphabet and interestingly an attempt at her own name as she wrote 'Alloo' on the back

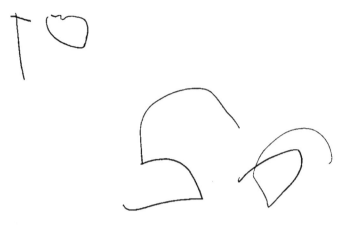

Figure 3.1 Alice's card

of the card. Already she recognised the need for five letters, an initial capital 'A' and then a 'l' followed by three other letters – which were not yet accurate. The achievement of the two key learning goals was being attained without any direct attention to those features. They were occurring within the context of children as active literacy learners.

So when children have the opportunity to engage with language and literacy, within this broad framework, at home and in early years settings, then the writing of their own name, and knowledge of the alphabet, can be learned very easily. It is learned because it develops as part of a wider experience with literacy activities. Practitioners in early years settings can support children by providing such learning opportunities that complement activities at home or provide new experiences for some children who have not had those literacy activities at home. Then because own name and alphabet are not simply taught directly, but are part of a much wider learning that learning is more firmly based and understood.

How will the literacy learning goals be achieved?

Because the writing of one's own name and knowledge of the letters and sounds of the alphabet appear to be two easily contained items, there might be a temptation to think of these being taught directly to the children by the teacher. For instance, David *et al.* (2000) noted in some UK observations that some of the nursery literacy activities that had been provided had been adult-led and adult-directed. They included using worksheets, activity cards and reading schemes rather than providing a range of opportunities for the children to explore and play with literacy. Worksheets are seldom the best way of teaching literacy and are unnecessary for young children when stories, play and nursery rhymes, etc. can provide a firmer basis for learning. As David *et al.* suggested, 'systematic and explicit "instruction" is inappropriate during the early years' (ibid.: 46). Indeed, if own name and the alphabet are taught directly, it appears that the children have an insufficient background to support their literacy development. Children who have the opportunity to play, sing and use language creatively have the basis for making rapid development with literacy as they move on through the early years (Mills and Mills 1998). Furthermore, it is that children *want* to read that is important and, as a Northern Ireland curriculum document indicated, 'The disposition to read is encouraged by reading rather than by instruction in how to read' (CCEA 1999: 9).

So we need to use the broad range of literacy experiences suggested above as a means of supporting the writing of one's own name and knowledge of the letters and sounds of the alphabet. Fortunately young children appear to be naturally interested in writing their own forename. Perhaps that should not surprise us. As children learn about who they are and how they can be represented in pictures and print, they naturally want to learn for themselves how to write their forename. In many of the studies of young children developing as literacy users before attending school, we read of the attempts of Giti, Cecilia, Adam and Alice to write their own name at about three years of age (e.g. Baghban 1984; Payton 1984; Schickedanz 1990; Campbell 1999). That suggests that writing materials and support for children's own attempts to write are provided by the adults. In one study I noted that early years settings provided a wide range of opportunities for young children to recognise and write their forename. Those included names on coat pegs for recognition, name cards collected at the beginning of the day and at other times, a class birthday chart, an alphabet book of class names, and tapping out the syllables of own name. The children were also encouraged to write their name by signing a register list, writing their own name on paintings, drawings and notes, and creating their own name with different media. Implicit in all of those activities was the encouragement to the child to write their own name frequently and for a purpose (Campbell 2001c). So the children were encouraged and supported to write their own name rather than being directly taught to do so, and they achieved that goal.

In the same way, when considering the alphabet, Strickland suggested that 'the best practice is to help children identify letters in an enjoyable way as they acquire the broader concepts about print and books' (1998: 56–7). She then provided a list of activities that started with a 'focus on letters that have special meaning for children, such as the letters in their own names. This is more effective than simply teaching one arbitrary letter per week' (ibid.: 57). So own name and alphabet are linked as the letters of the children's names provide a focus for considering the alphabet. Creating an alphabetic word wall with the children's names is usually of interest to the children. There are few classes that do not have at least two children with the same initial letter. That immediately provides an interest as the names are compared. Some practitioners add to that by including some of the favourite book characters on to the list. So from our examples above, Mary, Slinki Malinki, Owl, and Sam might be added to the word wall to add to the first letter comparisons.

Of course children learn about the alphabet as they explore the writing of their own name. For instance, Giti, Cecilia, Adam and Alice would have a good knowledge of the letters of their own name as they developed to the accurate writing of their forename over a number of months. Then the alphabetic word wall of children's names and characters from stories extends that knowledge. Additionally singing the alphabet song, typically to the tune of 'Twinkle-twinkle little star', help children to learn the names of letters and the alphabet sequence (Campbell 2002). When an adult uses an alphabet chart to point to the letters on occasions during that singing, then letter recognition is encouraged. All that is done as part of an enjoyable adult–children interaction, the letters are learned incidentally as part of that process. Making an alphabet book of the environmental print links to the earlier suggestions of activities with that print, it also supports developing knowledge of the alphabet. There are also many attractive alphabet books, such as *Animalia* (Base 1986), that can be shared with the children. *Animalia*, for instance, contains alliterations for each letter of the alphabet focused on various animals. The children enjoy hearing about the animals and they learn about letter sounds as they enjoy the alliterations. A collection of alphabet books in the library corner for the children to look at extends the literacy learning and knowledge of the alphabet.

So the children write their own name and gain knowledge of the alphabet as part of a wider-based literacy provision. Nevertheless, they do specifically experience those two literacy activities supported by the teacher and other adults although not by direct teaching. Nevertheless the adults have an important role to play.

What are the roles of the adults in promoting literacy learning?

If the practitioner is not directly teaching, because that is not the most developmentally appropriate practice for young children, then what will be the role of practitioners and other adults in promoting the literacy learning? That question has already been answered in part as we have noted that the adult will read, model, demonstrate, interact, scaffold and support, sing, talk and inform (Campbell 1996). So the adult is very involved in ensuring that the children engage with literacy and become literacy users. And those roles have to be performed with skill and thought. For instance, when a story is read, the adult has to know the book, read at an appropriate pace and read with expression. Trelease (1995) suggested that reading too quickly is the most common mistake when reading aloud. When all that is achieved, a model of reading is provided for the children to help with their learning. During a shared reading there is a demonstration of reading including how the print is used. And when words are written on to a word wall it is writing that is demonstrated. In both of those demonstrations the adult interacts with the children so that there is an opportunity for the children to comment, question and respond. The interactions continue as the adult sings with the children and talks with them about environmental and classroom print. More specifically when children attempt to write their own name the adults assist as they scaffold, support and inform, thus direct teaching is only a very small part of the range of teaching skills used.

All that is made evident when we look at how Adam (Schickedanz 1990) and Alice (Campbell 1999) attained the goal of writing own name. They both did so before attending school. They did so because they were surrounded by literacy, with books read to them and familiar books repeated. They had adults who talked with them about what they were trying to achieve. And they had numerous opportunities provided for writing whenever they wanted. When they began to write their own name the adults supported them but accepted a learning process that lasted some months. From the first single 'A' to the eventual accurate name, each child was actively engaged in working out what was needed. The adult was there to scaffold, support and inform but did not feel it necessary to dictate what should occur. The outcome was a secure knowledge of writing one's own name by three and half years of age. It is a replication of that provision, support and encouragement in early years settings that helps other children to achieve those goals.

Conclusion

It is important that young children are enabled to write their own name and know the letter shapes by name and sound. The adults need to support that learning but to do so without concentrating on teaching those goals directly. Early years practitioners feel pressure being exerted by various government initiatives towards more direct teaching (David *et al.* 2000). Yet in England the *Curriculum Guidance for the Foundation Stage* (QCA 2000) does indicate for literacy learning that the practitioner needs, in relation to various literacy activities, to 'provide opportunities, encourage, talk about, play games, model, and sing etc.' (ibid.: 61). It is developmentally appropriate to use a variety of strategies linked to the children's interests and needs rather than attempt to teach particular learning goals directly. As we noted, learning needs to be the product of a wide range of activities and opportunities. The attention given to own name writing and alphabet knowledge is part of that much wider provision. Thus that specific learning is not neglected but rather becomes part of far more broad-based literacy foundations. It is a base from which children's literacy development can continue to thrive.

CHAPTER 4

The essence of history in the early years

Rosie Turner-Bisset

Introduction: two experiences of history

Four-year-old Thomas is on his grandfather's lap. They are looking at a family album. Thomas chatters and points to a picture of himself as a baby. 'That's me!' he said, 'and that's me in my high chair, and that's me with my train.' They continue through the album; then Grandad pulls out another album he brought with him to his daughter's house. 'Was this the olden days?' asked Thomas, as they peer at the smaller black and white prints of his Grandad in army uniform, in a suit on his wedding day, and in casual clothes holding up a darts trophy. Grandad says, 'Yes,' and he explains why he had his uniform on and what he was doing in each picture. Thomas points to a picture of his mother as a baby and says, 'Look, there's me again!' His Grandad gently explains that is not Thomas, but his mother as a baby. 'Of course it's me!' exclaimed Thomas. His Grandad points out that she is wearing a long robe and that pictures of Thomas show him in 'babygros', dungarees or shorts. 'She looks just like me!' said Thomas, and it is true: there is a marked resemblance.

The following day, in a classroom in the school where Thomas attends the nursery, his older sister, six-year-old Emma, is working with pictures and text. The teacher has told the story of 'Rapunzel' and her group have drawn four pictures of different parts of the story. Emma chose to draw the couple with their new baby, the witch taking the baby, the witch climbing up Rapunzel's hair and the prince falling into the prickly bush. For each picture she has to write a sentence underneath to explain what is happening in the picture. When she has finished, the teacher asks her to arrange the pictures in the sequence in which the events happened. She does this quickly, talking all the time about the story, using the time word 'then'. The rest of the group are still working on the pictures and writing; so the teacher asks, to extend Emma's thinking, to arrange the pictures into a different sequence and retell the story. Emma is very puzzled, but tries nonetheless. She puts the prince in the bush first, the couple with the baby next, the witch climbing up the hair third and the witch taking the baby last. 'That's not right!' says Emma, but her teacher persists and asks her what the story is now. 'Once upon a time there was a prince stuck in a bush,' prompts the teacher and continues with a different story based on the pictures in the new sequence. Emma gazes at her open-mouthed.

Both of these children were doing history. At first glance, it would seem that the first example is just a cosy family interaction between an older carer and a child, and the second example is of a literacy hour activity. Nonetheless, both examples contain elements of history: not only that, they are examples of good practice in doing history with the very young. To understand this, and to generate one's own good practice, a practitioner needs a complete understanding of the nature of history, and how that might be made accessible to children in the early years. The early years setting might seem to be far distant from the concerns of academic historians, but an understanding of their conceptions of history is fundamental to good practice in teaching history at whatever level. Thus this chapter contains: (i) a brief discussion of the nature of history; (ii) a 'Map of History' to guide understanding and practice; (iii) theories about children's learning related to history; (iv) examples of poor and good practice in early years history; and (v) some concluding ideas on the place of history in the early years curriculum. In a chapter of this length, I can do no more than sketch out examples of good practice based on theoretical underpinnings. Readers will find it useful to consult Turner-Bisset (2000) in which I give examples of learning activities involving artefacts, stories and play. This chapter introduces a wider range of activities intended to develop the skills, processes, and concepts of history, as well as positive attitudes towards it.

The essence of history

Historians will always debate the exact nature of their subject and there is not space to deal with those debates in this chapter; however, knowledge of a few key ideas about history are extremely useful for teaching it at any level, including the early years. I have written elsewhere that 'History is the imaginative reconstruction of the past, using what evidence we can find'(Turner-Bisset 2000: 171). We examine evidence from the past and state what we definitely know from the evidence. Much historical evidence, especially from the more distant past, is incomplete, and we have to hypothesise about it. We also use other experience and knowledge to inform our interpretations. Finally, we imagine how the past might have been, and reconstruct it in a variety of forms. Thus history is in part a creative activity. Collingwood (1994) suggested that historical evidence had something in common with the evidence used in a murder mystery: thus historians are like detectives, working out what might have happened from a range of clues and sources. Hexter (1972) introduced the useful notions of the first and second records. The first record is the visible, tangible evidence of the past: literally what remains, whether it is a fragment of Roman hypocaust or a Tudor lice-comb. The second record is all the knowledge and experience in one's life to date, which we bring to bear on the first record: if we have seen a hypocaust before or used a modern nit-comb, we can use that experience to work out what a piece of evidence might be and what it tells us about people at that time. Trevelyan (1913) wrote that history was composed of three aspects: (i) the scientific aspect of finding and examining the surviving evidence; (ii) the poetic/imaginative aspect of reconstructing past events and lives using the fragmentary evidence; and (iii) the literary/artistic aspect of communicating historical understanding.

As well as these ideas about history, the early years practitioner can draw upon a simple map of history in order to inform planning, teaching and assessing in this subject. The 'map of history' in Figure 4.1 shows history subject knowledge as being composed of three aspects: (i) substantive knowledge, or the substance of history; (ii) syntactic knowledge or the skills and processes of history; and (iii) beliefs and atittudes about history (Turner-Bisset 2001). The terms 'substantive' and 'syntactic'come from Schwab (1964, 1978). All subjects have their facts and concepts which go to make up the discipline, or its substance. In addition, there are a number of organising frameworks which help us to marshall those facts and concepts so that they are related and not just an indiscriminate mass of facts and ideas. The frameworks include the overarching concepts of the subject, which are listed for history in the left-hand column of Figure 4.1. In the middle column is the syntactic knowledge: the processes and skills that historians use in finding out about the past, or establishing new truths in the subject. The last column is just as important as the other two: what we believe a subject to be, and how we feel about it, will influence how we teach it. If for example, we believe that history is about memorising facts and dates we will teach it that way. If one feels history to be interesting and exciting, one will try to provide appropriate activities for children and communicate one's enthusiasm and excitement. The 'map of history' can be used to guide one's teaching and to create learning activities. For example, a walk with five-year-olds investigating street furniture can teach observation skills and concepts of 'old' and 'new'. Examining a metal plaque with crossed scissors on it set into a pavement can encourage the children to ask questions about why it is there and what it is for.

Children's learning in history

Our understanding of the subject knowledge of history needs to be linked to our understanding of children's learning, in order to generate meaningful activities for them. It is useful to consider briefly some key theories in relation to learning history. These theories are: schema theory (Piaget 1959); a conceptual change theory of learning; Bruner's (1970) ideas of different modes of mental representation; and Vygotsky's theories of social learning (1978). There are other theories which are of value, but these four can be most useful to us.

It is important to note that the schema theory outlined here is that of the Genevan school of psychologists, not the fascinating work on children's schema developed by Athey (1990) and described in Bruce (1997). This is not to say that there are no links between the two sets of ideas, but that for the purposes of understanding children's learning in history, schema theory can be extremely valuable. The key notion of

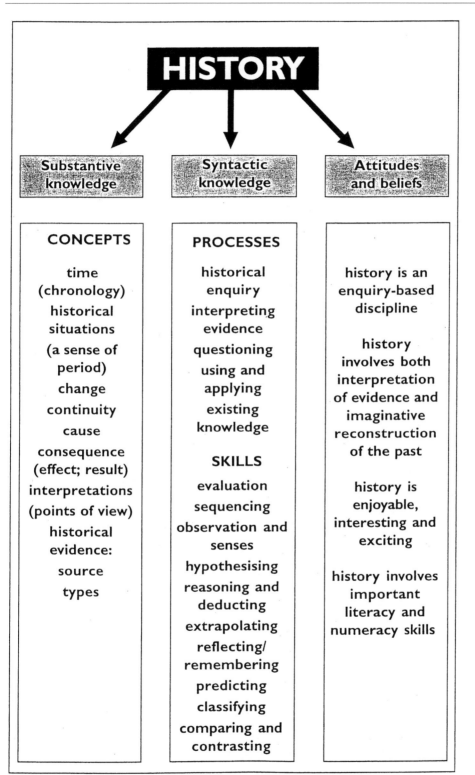

HISTORY

Substantive knowledge	Syntactic knowledge	Attitudes and beliefs
CONCEPTS time (chronology) historical situations (a sense of period) change continuity cause consequence (effect; result) interpretations (points of view) historical evidence: source types	**PROCESSES** historical enquiry interpreting evidence questioning using and applying existing knowledge **SKILLS** evaluation sequencing observation and senses hypothesising reasoning and deducting extrapolating reflecting/ remembering predicting classifying comparing and contrasting	history is an enquiry-based discipline history involves both interpretation of evidence and imaginative reconstruction of the past history is enjoyable, interesting and exciting history involves important literacy and numeracy skills

Figure 4.1 A map of history (Turner-Bisset, 2001) *Source*: Reproduced with permission from *Teaching History*, February 2001.

schema theory is that thought processes depend upon our ability to create mental representations of objects and people. The experiences we have are stored as part of our schema: complex patterns of internal representation which involve recognition, understanding, action and sometimes emotional reactions. Schemas are changed by the process of adaptation, which has two aspects: 'assimilation' and 'accommodation'. When a child has a new experience, some sort of image or internal representation is made of it: this is 'assimilation'. For the new experience to become part of one's schema, one has to work on the new ideas or information. This is called 'accommodation', and the process by which this happens is called 'equilibration'. In a state of disequilibrium one may feel emotion, pleasurable or otherwise: laughter, surprise, joy, fear, anger or inadequacy. Sometimes people ignore new information or experiences which do not accord with our existing schema. Some people choose to live with the conflict or disequilibrium, which can be rather uncomfortable. In learning, people restructure their schemas to accommodate new information, ideas, or experience. This restructuring is the process of accommodation. The learner has to take an active part in this process. In history, through interaction with adult carers, the children's existing second record (Hexter 1972), which forms part of their schema, is altered through the experience of doing history. Thus in our first example in this chapter, Thomas is learning that not all pictures of babies are of himself and that background information in a photograph or picture can give clues to identity. His learning was accompanied by the feeling of surprise as he explored the new notion that the older baby picture was not of himself. At first he was inclined to reject the new idea which did not fit into his mental map, schema or second record. Only through continued interaction and examination of the photograph did he come to accommodate the new idea.

Learning may also be viewed as a process of concept acquisition and conceptual change. The process of learning to name and classify the people, creatures and objects with whom they come into contact, can be gradual. For example, a child may see several large four-legged creatures with tails and udders and see many pictures of such animals, before learning that they are all cows. History is packed with concepts, some of which are simple, but many of which are abstract and these must be actively taught over a period of time. Thus in the early years, teachers need to recognise that learning language and concepts are closely related: children have to use and understand terms like 'very old', 'old' and 'new' over a period of time and in relation to different objects, buildings and people, to build up their understanding of such concepts.

Bruner's (1970) notion of mental representations is extremely powerful for early years teaching. In this theory he stated that there were three characteristic ways of understanding the world. There are three forms of mental representation of what we encounter in the real world. The first is enactive representation, or understanding by experience and doing. The second is iconic representation, or understanding through pictures, diagrams and drawings. The third is symbolic representation or understanding through some kind of symbol system. Examples of systems are language, both spoken and written, mathematical notation and musical notation. Young children use enactive representations first, then iconic ones, moving into symbolic representations as they get older. Thus a child might play at going on holiday in the nursery, draw herself going on holiday in reception class, and write about her holiday in Year 2. Adults move back and forth between different forms of representation. Thus for young children, enactive representations of historical ideas or information can be more powerful and effective modes of teaching than those that involve symbolic representation. Ultimately our aim is to have children learning using all three modes of representation.

One idea from Vygotsky's (1978) theories of social learning can be particularly helpful for the early years. He introduced the notion of 'the zone of proximal development': the potential for learning, understanding, knowing and doing which is not yet realised, but which can be realised through interaction with others. Thus Thomas was unable to make sense of his Grandad's photo album on his own, but through social interaction with a more knowledgeable adult, was able to do so. Emma was perhaps too young to understand abstract concepts of cause and effect, but through the sequencing activities provided by her teacher, she was offered an opportunity to begin to comprehend the relationship between the chronology of events and cause and effect. If you change the order of the pictures, you change the events and their relationship to each other. By her intervention, Emma's teacher was trying to extend Emma's learning and challenge her thinking. If these theories of learning are related to the ideas of Hexter (1972), they provide a powerful justification for the kind of active whole class, pair and group teaching which characterises the best practice in history teaching. For example, a group of five- and six-year-olds investigating old artefacts first thought that a pottery hot water bottle was for keeping money in. One child had seen one very similar on her granny's hearth. She suggested that it might be a hot water bottle: the children discussed pouring in the water, and what it might feel like to have the hard pottery against one's toes in bed (Turner-Bisset 2000). Children can add to the second records or schema of other children through pair and group interaction, and one of the key roles of adults in early years history teaching is to extend the children's second records, by sharing their own with them.

Knowledge of and use of a number of theories about children's learning have implications for teaching approaches. Through understanding theories of learning, we see the need for a wide range of teaching approaches, which use all three forms of representation in teaching.

Good practice in early years history

This section is prefaced with an example of poor practice in teaching history, intended to stand in sharp contrast to the good examples and to emphasise how history should *not* be taught. The example is from a final year BEd student on teaching placement in a Year 1 class. When interviewed as part of a research study into beliefs and practice in teaching primary history, she explained the context in which she tried to operate her own philosophy of teaching early years history:

> I had a bit of a nightmare topic: it was so big and vague. It was basically 2000 years of history in a term which was going to cover from the beginning of time through to the Millennium Dome, and I had to slot in. This was a Year 1 class of which about six or seven of the children had only had a term in reception. It was a very young class and I really felt that trying to cover two thousand years with these children was a little bit inappropriate. I observed one of her sessions where the teacher taught the Anglo-Saxons in two weeks, in two thirty-minute lessons. I felt the whole thing was just ludicrous because you could see it going straight over the children's heads; they were so young. They had no concept of the Anglo-Saxons or when they lived. She used a video, which she said she would use again, but I felt it was a bit old for them. They liked colouring the picture. So I decided that the best thing for me was to focus on one period; so I fixed on the Victorian times. I decided to teach it through story and artefact and that was my approach. (Celia, final year BEd student)

Before she was able to teach her lessons, she had the opportunity to observe a supply teacher with this class. Her teacher had an accident and was off for three weeks:

> There was a big muddle when she was off; so a supply teacher took over. When he asked what we were doing, I said the Victorians. He latched on to inventions and did a session, and I could see it just didn't do a thing: the children could not relate to it. He also had a picture of a modern sitting room and a Victorian sitting room for them to find the differences. They couldn't do it. They were just not mature enough, or did not have the ability. They didn't understand that they did not have a television in Victorian times; they couldn't see the difference between gas lights and electric lights. I didn't see any learning but, again, they liked colouring the picture. (Celia, final year BEd student)

It is important to state what is wrong with these two examples, because by doing so we can begin to understand what is appropriate for children of this age. Among the issues for discussion are: having appropriate expectations; young children's understanding of time; issues of children's learning of time language, and of concepts such as Anglo-Saxon or Victorian; the kinds of teaching methods used; and whether we can have such young children realistically doing any more than 'colouring the picture'. The class teacher was caught up with adult concerns (celebration of the Millennium) and did not consider how meaningless this might be to children who are still struggling to use 'yesterday' and 'tomorrow' correctly. If it is hard for us as adults to comprehend the concept of two thousand years of history, how much harder is it for the very young, who may only have five or six years on which to draw as an understanding of time? The topic of the Millennium was totally inappropriate for this reason. Sadly, this was not an isolated case. That year I had at least ten students, out of a cohort of one hundred, coming to me in a panic, asking how to cope with teaching the Millennium to Reception, Year 1 or Year 2. This kind of topic encourages the worst practice in history teaching, in which the Romans, Tudors or Vikings get a couple of brief lessons and the children are rushed on to the next topic without any consideration of whether or not they have learned anything. It also flies in the face of, for example, Bruce's ten core principles of early childhood education and care, one of which is 'What children can do (rather than what they cannot do) is the starting point of a child's education' (Bruce 1997: 97).

Expecting children of this age to understand concepts of two thousand years, or of 'Anglo-Saxons' without teaching approaches which incorporate enactive representations of difficult concepts, betrays a lack of understanding of children's learning and a paucity of teaching approaches. Research evidence on children's understanding of time across primary and secondary education, admirably summed up by Stowe and Haydn (2000), suggests that the complex concept of time, bound up with mathematical, linguistic and logical areas of understanding, develops gradually over a long period of time and at differing rates in different people. As adults we are constantly refining our concept of time. Other considerations are that the development of the concept of time is inextricably bound up with proficiency in language, and that we make it difficult for pupils because we have a wide range of different systems for describing time: dates; time span words such as 'decade', location by event ('when Mummy was born'); terms for large but inexact amounts of time such as 'aeon'; and for smaller, more precise units of time or periods ('Tudor') (Wood 1995: 11). Stowe and Haydn (2000) suggest using visual representations to teach time, such as pictures to sequence and they add that very young children may find it easier to compare, say, a Roman dwelling with a modern one, rather than a Victorian one, because they find it easier to distinguish the more distant past.

An enactive representation of time such as a time line using children as physical markers for different periods, done to scale using perhaps the school playground can communicate the idea of large amounts of time through the visual and physical distance between markers. Much early years practice is concerned with language development and our teaching of time and change should focus on developing understanding and usage of simple time vocabulary and concepts. Thus learning the days of the week, and months of the year, and sequencing events using these is dealing with fundamental historical concepts and processes. Personal time lines, or time lines related to events well known to a group of children can be useful too. The example of Thomas looking at photos of himself from when he was a baby up to four years, and then looking at the older photos of his family is good practice in teaching about time and change on a one-to-one basis. The essential historical skill to be learned and practised is sequencing, which is what the teacher was encouraging Emma to do in the second example. Sequencing is a skill which is found across the curriculum, for example, in maths, language, music, PE and dance. Thus to sequence a series of pictures and captions experienced within a literacy hour is to practise a historical skill. If, like Emma's teacher, one challenges the child to change the sequence, one can see what impact changing the order of events has on a story, and hence begin to work long-term to relating chronology to cause and effect.

The example of poor practice has been discussed at length as a means of introducing notions of good practice. Teaching approaches are all-important, along with a deep understanding of the nature of history, of children in the early years, and of how they learn. To be able to move away from the ubiquitous video-watching and colouring of pictures, one needs to make substantive knowledge, or historical content less important, and syntactic knowledge, or the skills and processes of history, more important, in planning, teaching and assessing. One can refer to Figure 4.1 as a means of planning for teaching history even for very young children. The historical concepts in substantive knowledge in Figure 4.1 are to be taught gradually, incrementally over a long period of time, as children will develop their understanding of these at differing rates. They can be incorporated into teaching the syntactic knowledge, or skills and processes, some of which are specific to history and some of which, such as observation or recording, are generic skills, to be found across the curriculum. Instead of the teacher asking 'What do I want my children to know about the Anglo-Saxons?', and attempting to teach content through video, the question becomes 'What skills and processes do I want to develop in my children?' This accords with the notion of the process curriculum, as promulgated by Blenkin and Kelly (1996) as being suitable for early years education.

An example of good practice

It follows that with a full understanding of the nature of history, and of the integrated nature of learning in the early years, one can comprehend how history can be taught throughout the early years curriculum, in the Foundation Stage and in Key Stage 1, not just under the obvious area of learning of 'Knowledge and understanding of the world' but as part of the other five areas of learning. (QCA 2000) The five- and six-year-olds examining the pottery hot-water bottle (Turner-Bisset 2000) handled it with care, because it was heavy and might break. They took turns to hold and feel it. They communicated their understanding in oral language, pictures and writing. As a teacher, I could have extended the activity into mathematical and scientific learning by inviting them to predict how much water we would need to fill it, and letting them fill it, with cold water of course. In another example children in the nursery played at going on holiday (Miller 2000). In doing so they engaged in physical play of packing, and communication in their sharing of their second records of holiday experiences, pooled to create the new experience in the imaginative play.

The next example of good practice comes from some work done in a year 1 class in a suburban school, with three or four ethnic minority children and a traveller child whose attendance was erratic. The aim was to develop a 'history mystery' for the early years. Other development work has been done, notably by Nichol (1999) on creating history mysteries for Key Stage 2, but the challenge was to create learning activities and materials suitable for early years. Since history is fundamentally about people, I decided to use people and characters in my teaching. For resources, I drew upon the very nearly free 'Mr Men' characters, given away by a well-known burger chain. I knew that at least some of the children would know some of the characters as the books were available in the classroom and many would have eaten at the burger restaurants. I was trying to start from what they would know. A murder mystery was not suitable for young children, so I devised instead a story in which Mr Happy baked himself a birthday cake which then disappeared from his table by the window. This drew upon work the previous term when the children had baked a cake and iced it. Prior to this we had done some preliminary work on characters, with the children discussing as a class on the carpet, each character as she or he was pulled out of my special bag. They then recorded their understanding of the characters through differentiated work.

The following day I introduced them to the mystery and to eight of the characters who had been in the area at the time. Using their knowledge of the characters they had to reason which of the eight it might have been. I had intended only to practise the use of the connective 'because' and to develop the processes of reasoning from the evidence, but these five- and six-year-olds were soon using conditional tenses with ease in spoken language, because of the demands of hypothesising. Figures 4.2 and 4.3 show Jed's work (one of the most able children) and Nazia's work. Jed had to write his own version of the story and complete the sentence showing his conclusion. Nazia had the text of the story printed as a book to be illustrated. Her group read this page by page with the classroom assistant and drew pictures. They then either independently, or with the assistant writing, had to write their conclusion. It was interesting that they both came to the same conclusion.

In the final lesson, we shared the story again, discussed the mystery, the children finished the work and I told them what had really happened. Together we worked out what we would need to do to make Mr Happy happy again. All the lessons were conducted within the framework of the Literacy Hour. In the plenary we shared work and learnt a folk song, orally, about a young girl going to meet her man, and the clothing she wore, which was a way of learning about what people wore in Victorian times (that term's topic). This could be extended and consolidated by providing dressing up materials which matched the song.

Conclusion

The previous example is of good practice in teaching history, and for that matter literacy, for the mystery provided a genuine context for extended speaking and listening, reading and writing. What was being learnt here were some of the skills and processes of history: questioning, enquiry, interpreting evidence ('It could not have been Mr Rush because he would not have stopped rushing!' said Tom), using and applying existing knowledge, hypothesising, reasoning and deducting and remembering, of the plot of the story. The children enjoyed creating their illustrated books and showed them off proudly. They engaged in personal and social development

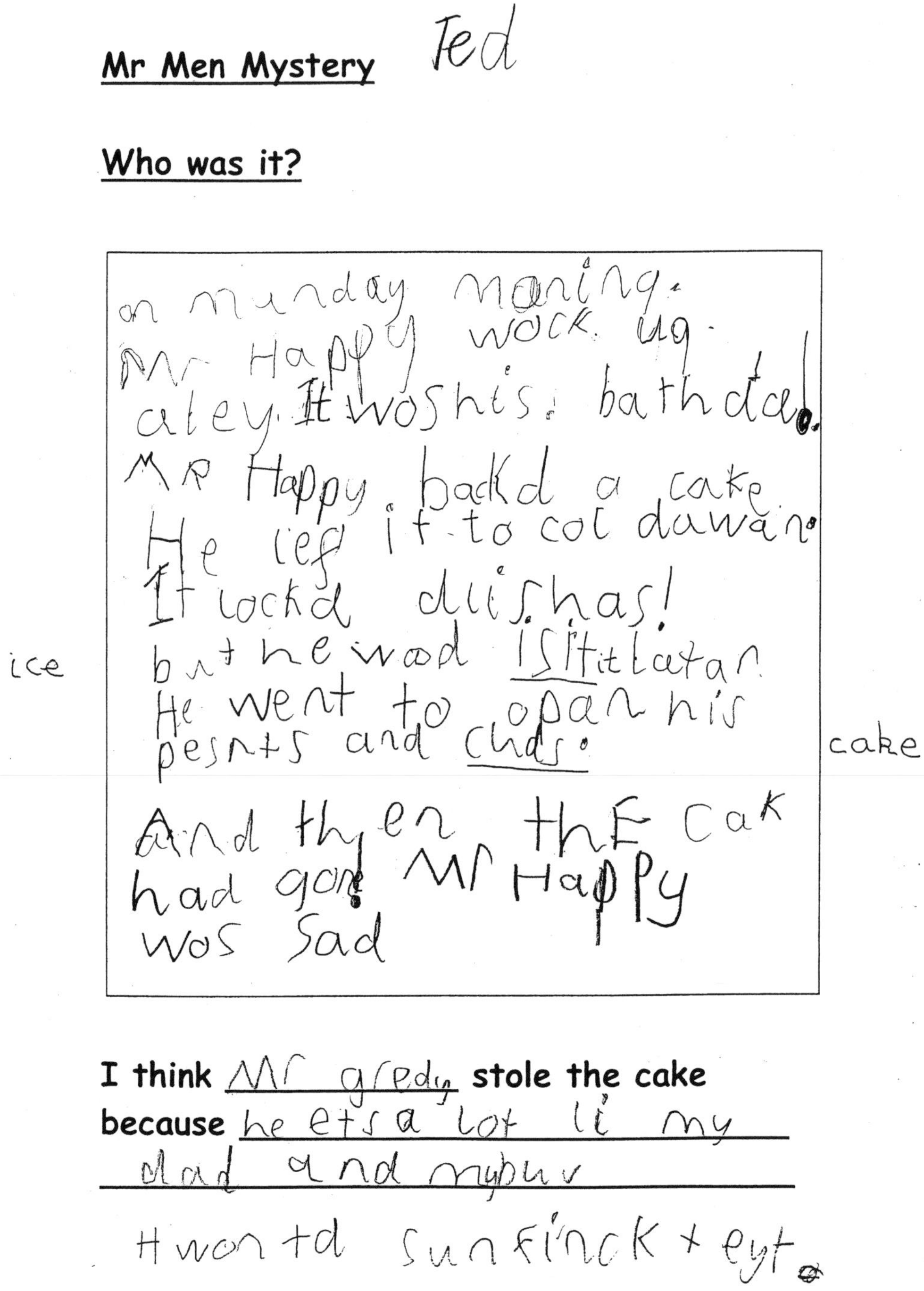

Mr Men Mystery *Jed*

Who was it?

on munday moning.
mr Happy wock up.
aley. It wos his. bath dae.
Mr Happy backd a cake
He lef it to col dawn
It lockd duishas!
but he wood isititlatan
He went to opan his
pesnts and chds

ice

cake

And then thE cak
had gone Mr Happy
wos sad

I think Mr gredy stole the cake
because he ets a lot li my
dad and mybuv
H won td sun finck t eyt.

Figure 4.2 Jed's work.

When he came back, it was gone. Mr.
Happy cried. He was sad now.

Who stole the birthday cake?

I thik it was
Mr greedy because he
is always hungry and he
liks to eat cake.

Figure 4.3 Nazia's work

through the consideration of Mr Happy's feelings and how we could restore his happiness. Viewed in this way, as skills, processes and attitudes, it is possible to see how important history can be to the early years curriculum, for some of the syntactic knowledge central to the learning and teaching of history can be found across the curriculum. Early years practitioners need to develop their understanding of the essence of history, and relate this to their knowledge of young children learning. With the deep understanding outlined in this chapter, one can create opportunities for historical learning in activities which at first glance, might seem to have more to do with literacy or play.

This chapter has introduced a wide range of ideas and issues on: the nature of history; theories about children's learning related to history; examples of poor and good practice in early years history; and some concluding ideas on the place of history in the early years curriculum. It is not possible in a chapter of this length to give more examples of good practice, but readers are urged to consult Cooper (1995) and Wood and Holden (1995) for an abundance of ideas for teaching history in the early years. Above all, history is enjoyable, interesting and exciting: through the activities we devise, we communicate the essential nature of history, take children forward from what they can do and understand, and give pleasure through doing so.

CHAPTER 5

Drawing as a language in the early years

Rosemary Allen

Introduction

This chapter explores how drawing acts as an important form of language in the early years. The relationships between reading, writing, drawing and speaking are discussed and are shown to be part of an intricate system of human functions, governed by a complex and highly sophisticated symbiosis of mind and body.

Knowledge of how learning takes place within the creative areas enables adults to strengthen the framework within which they address young children's learning needs. Theoretical structures that support the whole child are discussed. Drawing is seen as central to healthy physical, emotional and cognitive development and is the foundation of visual thinking, providing opportunities for meeting challenges, finding solutions and taking risks with ideas. Understanding drawing as a language rather than regarding it as an immature form of communication to be left behind as quickly as possible, helps adults to see it as a legitimate concern and to invest in its growth and development. Clearly, this has important implications for early years practitioners

Frameworks for creative development

In the early years, learning can be grouped into areas that mirror the way humans behave and develop their thought processes. From birth, people experience the world and communicate with others through movement, sight and sound. Parents and other carers know the importance of engaging with babies and young children in ways that encourage them to learn to make sounds which when repeated become tunes, rhythms and eventually words, sentences and songs; to copy simple movements which become increasingly complex and elaborate, evolving into games and dances; to effect arm and hand movements that can make marks on surfaces; to select patterns, textures, objects and colours, that later become paintings, drawings, collages and structures. Selleck (1997) calls this early stage 'baby art' and describes its significant role in the expression of emotion and communication with others.

These early experiences lay the foundations for children's understanding of themselves and the wider world, with speaking, singing, soundmaking, drawing, construction and movement rapidly emerging as primary modes of expression (Duffy 1998).

Our current views of what constitutes good practice in creative development, the learning area within which drawing is usually considered, owe much to the collective research on children and learning over the past 150 years. It has established that children's needs are best met through a wide range of experiences based on sound knowledge of child development. The early years are a platform for children's healthy physical and mental growth and their happiness and well-being are regarded as important ingredients in their educational experiences. While there have been criticisms of this flexible, creative approach to learning which contrasted sharply with the narrow, controlled style of interaction inherited from Victorian times, there is widespread agreement that it is appropriate at least in the early years. Even the current emphasis on numeracy and literacy, enshrined within the structure of the Foundation Stage guidance (QCA 2000), the National Curriculum (DfEE/QCA 1999) and defined by the National Literacy Strategy (DfEE 1998a) and the National Numeracy Strategy (DfEE 1999b), does not challenge the notion that a broad curriculum, imaginatively delivered, with due regard to the natural rhythms of human development, not only provides a framework for the healthy development of individuals but also for society (Bruce 1987).

It is not difficult to see that the creative and expressive curriculum for the early years has an impact across the whole of children's learning: cognitive, perceptual, physical, language, social and emotional. Duffy (1998) reminds us that these aspects of learning interact and overlap. Drawing itself has an important role within each of these domains, playing a vital part in human expression and communication. Indeed, the understanding of children's need for interrelated, creative, exploratory experiences formed the basis of the child-centred practice of such educational pioneers as Froebel, in the nineteenth century and Montessori and Steiner at the turn of the twentieth century. Practice was based on knowledge of child development taken from their own research and that of others in the field of child psychology and education. Despite differences in their methods, they had in common a strong belief in the value of childhood and the need for activities to take place in a nurturing and stimulating environment among adults who were committed to the needs of the whole child. Highly creative and imaginative approaches to learning were valued, with the arts seen as dominant features of the curriculum. Children were encouraged to draw freely and with imagination and expression, as the formal, copied style of the Victorian classroom was rejected. Such has been their impact on education, that there are currently many thriving Montessori and Steiner schools in Britain and Europe. In Britain many of these creative ideas reached their height in the 1960s and were enshrined in the influential Plowden Report (DES 1967). The current curriculum guidance for the foundation stage (QCA 2000) has drawn upon key research in emphasising the roles and responsibilities of adults in encouraging children to learn through play and first-hand exploration. The six interrelated areas of experience – personal, social and emotional development; communication, language and literacy; mathematical development; knowledge and understanding of the world; physical development; and creative development – aim to meet the whole child's diverse needs and the role of drawing across the curriculum is clearly acknowledged (QCA 2000).

The development of drawing

Drawing, in fact, is regarded as such a significant language form, particularly in the early years, that some have focused solely on this area of research. Lowenfeld and Brittain (1970), Kellogg (1969), Gardner (1980), Goodnow (1977), Cox (1997) and others have drawn upon the work of such influential psychologists as Piaget (1951), Bruner (1986), and Vygotsky (1986), in analysing the function and form of drawing as they relate to stages of development. These have been documented thoroughly by experts in the field over the past 80 years and their work provides us with fascinating information. What concerns us most here, however, is the degree to which drawing can be seen as a powerful and complex language in its own right and how it interacts, supports and drives the other systems of language.

In his long-term detailed investigation of children's drawing, Steele defines language as 'any symbolic system, coded or uncoded, which facilitates articulation, expression, and communication of perceptions, thoughts and feelings' (1998: 19). He draws parallels between the codes required for speech, writing and reading and those used for drawing, pointing to the increasing complexity of schema as evidence of vocabulary, style and syntax. Schema in the context of drawing are personal, repeated symbols for people, buildings, creatures, plants and other commonly drawn features including such abstract ideas as enclosure, speed or direction. They are the graphic equivalent of words and, like words, are similar to other children's symbols, although they often display individual variation. Most of us are familiar with a five-year-old's drawing of a person consisting of two circles with stick-like arms and legs, small circles for eyes and a curved line for the mouth. Although the child knows that a person does not really look like this, it is a universal symbol that crosses the boundaries of time and culture (Cox 1997). Parallels exist with written languages across the world in that they share similarities of letter formation and structure (Gardner 1980). Some written forms of language, for example, Chinese, derive directly from the original drawn symbols for the meaning of the word. Societies develop shared schema as a kind of shorthand for information on street signs and maps. We even invent our own adult schema in repeated personal doodles that we make often while thinking quietly or conversing with others. Thus we can begin to see that drawn and written characters are similar, interrelated systems of communication. Edwards (1988) maintains that not only pictures but also simple marks can be read like a language. The qualities of a line can convey subtle meaning in the way that it is drawn, just as the same word may be spoken in a range of ways, indicating to the listener a different meaning according to pitch, tone, speed or context. In fact, people are generally very skilful at reading meaning in expression, voice and body language. We even begin to make judgements about someone's character on the basis of handwriting or drawing style and are certainly able to tell how the piece has been executed, for example, speedily and roughly or carefully and thoughtfully.

Matthews (1994) and Steele (1998) have focused their research on drawing both as a language form and its support for the learning of literacy. Steele points out that drawing's immediacy, familiarity and fluency allow emergent readers and writers to express 'complex thoughts and feelings' that they are not yet able to express in words (1998: 19). Matthews shows how letters, words and sentences begin to emerge from drawings because writing and drawing use the same basic mark vocabulary and usually fulfil the same purpose, for example, a description of an action using words and images. He urges adults to look beyond what might appear to be meaningless scribble and to take part in an interactive game of sounds, mark making and conversation. For example, he describes how at 26 months Hannah synchronises her own speech sounds with a drawing of a series of horizontal arcs. The arc seems to be a representation of the sound and could be interpreted as 'writing'. Later when an adult joins in the vocalisation, Hannah seems to be 'writing down' the sounds in response to 'dictation' (1994: 89). Thus we begin to see the symbiosis between speaking and listening, drawing and writing.

Recent developments in the study of the brain demonstrate the interdependency of the functions of sight, hearing, sound and movement especially, but not exclusively, in the early years (Ratey 2001). Using this understanding it is easy to see that the creative aspects of learning – music, art and design, dance, imaginative play and narrative – have a central role in children's holistic development. Understanding that it is not simply the brain that drives the body, but a series of interrelated systems which link mind, body, environment together, has important implications for the ways in which the early years curriculum is organised and how adults care for and interact with children. This knowledge presents a challenge to the views of those who see these areas as an adjunct to 'proper' learning – to be reduced and finally dropped by all but the talented few as children progress through the education system.

Studies from around the world reveal that far from drawing being confined to those who are 'artistic', it is an important language form featuring regularly within the lives of individuals and of societies (Edwards 1988). Much of the information we gather about a culture is in the form of drawing and writing or, more commonly, a combination of the two. Whatever their country of origin, all children begin drawing with mark making and then progress in broadly similar patterns of development. Edwards (1992) and Ratey (2001) believe that there is compelling evidence to suggest that the brain is hardwired to learn to draw in the roughly same developmental stages, as it is to learn to speak.

Figure 5.1 'Bang!' Boy aged 2 years 1 month

Drawing is regularly accompanied by vocalisations – sliding sounds, dipping and diving sounds, humming and crashing sounds. Clearly sound, movement and early drawing are closely related, can 'tell a story' and represent meaning. These are language systems working in harmony. Frequently, meaning is associated with movement or function at this early stage. The word 'bang!' may be represented by sharp dots on paper applied with force and vigour as Figure 5.1 shows. Steele (1998) maintains that drawing acts as a kind of visual commentary on the inner self and the world, bringing together the physical, affective and cognitive domains. As children grow older they learn to shift from speaking aloud to an inner commentary that helps to clarify thinking and decision-making. Adults continue to use the inner voice throughout their lives for a range of purposes, for example, to fix directions for a journey in the memory, to rehearse an argument in a difficult meeting, or as part of their guiding intuition. It is the uninhibited talking to oneself that diminishes rather than the talking *per se*. We would do well to notice the importance of our own inner commentary in order to encourage and guide children in theirs.

Drawing as a language form

There can be few people familiar with young children who do not recognise drawing as a vital form of communication – a language through which movements can be traced, an idea articulated or problem thought through. If, as Steele (1998) argues, drawing is part of the foundation of communication with others, we should not regard it as inferior but should encourage children to learn the necessary skills in order to make progress. Although we may regard speech as a much more sophisticated and mature form of communication than drawing, in fact the two go hand in hand. Steele points out that vocabulary and syntax in language are replicated in drawing through the vocabulary of schema and the arrangement of ideas and thoughts. Ratey (2001) shows how the development of language – naming, describing and projecting – has parallels in drawing, thus it can be regarded as a form of writing, not the poor relation to it.

Young children's visual language of drawing serves largely the same function as spoken language and goes through a similar process in its development. Parallels can be drawn between simple mark making of dots, lines and swirls that eventually become symbols for objects, ideas or events with a range of sounds, which become syllables and then words and sentences. Thus scribbling and babbling can be seen as similar phases to be supported and encouraged on the basis of knowledge of the normal patterns of development in speech and drawing. Writing becomes part of this development – emerging from a combination of talking, reading and drawing. The mental processes that give rise to these actions are themselves influenced by the child's relationship with his or her environment including other people – families, friends and the wider community.

In the same way that soundmaking and then babbling are the result of being physically capable, drawing is the natural outcome of the ability to make whole body, arm, hand and finger movements. Having something to draw on and with becomes an essential part of this process and children abandon pens, which do not leave a mark in favour of mark-making implements (Berefelt 1987). In a similar way, young children rely on interaction with others in order to develop speech and even newborn babies can be observed engaging in sound conversations with their parents, first mimicking mouth shapes and then the sounds they give rise to. Matthews argues that scribbling and babbling are not merely mindless physical responses but that they also help to 'create a mood, or at least intensify an existing one' (1994: 18). Here we see the mind/body/environment connection. The physical pleasure of scribbling and the magic of making a mark can influence the brain's structures. The action and the mood are connected through neural pathways and the experience committed to memory to be retrieved later for more sensory pleasure and approval from adults (Ratey 2001).

Later as the repertoire of movements extends from side to side and up and down creating lines, to round and round creating circles, children make increasingly controlled joined-up shapes. These lines and shapes, together with dots and slashes seen in Figure 5.2 form the basis of the symbolic and expressive language of drawing. This complete language enables children to think about issues, record events, express an emotion, connect ideas, and deliver a message or to quiet the mind. The wider repertoire of marks also enables the child to combine shapes which then become symbols for familiar images such as people, trees, animals, buildings, leading to the visual equivalent of a story, description or an idea.

Tony's drawing of swimmers at the pool (Figure 5.3) uses several drawing conventions to describe the scene. As children begin to compose pictures, they also embark on the complex process of solving problems of communication through visual means. They use an evolving visual language base to help them express their ideas, which include:

Figure 5.2 A repertoire of marks; boy aged 2 years 11 months

Figure 5.3 A visit to the swimming pool; boy aged 6 years.

- the use of baselines to give stability and space, commonly used in landscapes and other scenes;
- x-ray drawings which show interiors and exteriors simultaneously, for example, ideas in heads, insides and outsides of buildings;
- fold-over drawings which are early solutions to perspective as in depictions of both sides of a street, or a circle of people;
- sequence drawings which show several stages of action such as comic book-style images;
- complex stories and themes both real and imagined, for example, dreams and imaginary stories. (Steele 1998: 37)

These increasingly detailed drawings deal with issues relating to the inner life of the child and his or her growing understanding of the world and along with other 'non-verbal messages remain an important form of communication throughout life' (QCA 2000: 45). Multi-sensory experiences will encourage the brain's flexibility and helps children to understand that languages are diverse and multifaceted and that issues can be dealt with in different ways and seen from different viewpoints. Such an approach makes the most of 'windows of opportunity' when the brain is primed to learn a particular function most effectively (Ratey 2001: 41). It is essential, therefore, that those engaging with young children should provide a different context for issues to be explored so that diversity of communication is emphasised and encouraged rather than narrowed and reduced to reading and writing.

The role of the adult in promoting drawing as a language

Motivating children to draw is not usually difficult as it is a regular feature of their repertoire. Its value as part of healthy physiological development means that simply by providing a range of opportunities to draw and plenty of encouragement, an adult can quickly set the scene for effective drawing development. Cox (1997) emphasises the importance of children sometimes drawing freely of their own voli- tion but reminds us that most will benefit from guidance as in reading and writing. Although a detailed understanding of child development is not essential to the pro- motion of drawing, it certainly helps to provide a supporting framework for effec- tive interaction between the child, the adult and the context (Beetlestone 1998). In babyhood and early infancy Matthews has shown that drawings are influenced by 'subtle responses from adults' in the form of careful listening, thoughtful prompts and conversations, whose interest can evoke a change of attitude or pace or may influence content and meaning (1994: 20). This contrasts with some earlier views of child art where adult interaction was thought to suppress children's natural crea- tivity (Cox 1997). This has largely given way to the knowledge that appropriate interactions with adults promote practical skills and enhance the child's understand- ing and knowledge of themselves and the wider world (Athey 1990; Clement *et al.* 1998; Cox 1997). Bruner's (1986) work on scaffolding and adult intervention and Vygotsky's (1986) concerns with the influence of social interaction on language and learning provide convincing arguments for regular attentive adult support as chil- dren's natural drawing development unfolds.

Keeping examples of children's drawings and taking photographs of them at work reveal evidence of the patterns of change, helping guide the adult in further inter- ventions relevant to the context. An observant adult will notice how children shape their own experiences, at times acting intuitively, other times controlling materials, ideas and feelings more deliberately. Even very young children are capable of acting on this 'dialogue' between intention and opportunity (Matthews 1994: 27) and it is here that discussion can play an important part in helping a child to make con- nections between areas of learning. Describing, commenting, encouraging using voice and body, all support the process of making meaning through drawing.

As learning becomes more formalised around the ages of 3 or 4, children are ready to learn through a more proactive approach. It is here that the adult can begin to guide the child, drawing attention to detail and making focused comments regard- ing the style of a drawing or method of making. Drawing will be focused mainly on storytelling, visual description, explanations and comparisons but at this stage the adult should encourage the skills of close observation through drawing. By the age of 6 this should include opportunities for more careful analysis of issues, ideas and objects through drawing using a range of materials. Most children by the age of 8 will be able to readily use a range of drawing systems to make drawings for differ- ent purposes.

Setting the scene for effective use of drawing

Figure 5.3 shows Tony aged 5, swimming at the local pool with his classmates. At first glance the figures are similar but on closer examination it is clear that there are subtle variations in the way they have been drawn that demonstrate Tony's observational skills and his ability to commit details to memory. He has developed his own schema for the swimmers, showing both movement and direction in the character of the lines and the placing of the drawing on the paper. His visual memory, aided by observation and his own experience of being a swimmer, has enabled him to depict the ways in which bodies move as they swim. He can even express the emotions of the individual swimmers ranging from excitement, concentration, dismay and confidence. The lines representing water tell us how it moves in response to the wave machine. It is a sophisticated image that far exceeds his ability to use the written or spoken word to describe the scene. His skilful and sensitive teacher knows the importance of discussion and he has talked with her about what he remembers and wants to record before beginning. The class looked at photographs of swimmers and swimming pools, discussing the sounds and smells they recalled. The teacher had audiotaped their last visit to the pool and played the tape recording to the class. They used musical instruments and moved their hands, arms and bodies to interpret some of the sounds. The children gathered around a large reproduction of a painting by Leon Kossoff of a busy swimming pool in the 1960s. They talked in pairs about their ideas for a picture before selecting a drawing tool and paper and making their drawing. When finished, the drawings were laid on the floor in a pavement show and everyone talked about the work before they were added to the display in the classroom. Some were pinned on the wall alongside key words identified by the children, while others became part of a class book about the visit and were accompanied by descriptive words and sentences. Thus the teacher and the adult helpers set the scene for learning at the planning stage and then made connections between the learning systems of the children and the curriculum areas. They made effective use of multi-sensory experiences, differentiating for a range of learning styles and giving the children opportunities to express their knowledge through art conversations, drawings, writing, movement and music.

In this description of an afternoon's work we can see adults giving value to children's drawings and enabling them to use the drawing process effectively to support 'joined-up' learning (Chisholm 2001). Setting the scene in this way requires thoughtful and willing adults who believe that drawing makes a fundamental contribution to the development of the whole child. Ongoing adult interest and focused input will ensure that the child perceives drawing and related activities to be as important as speaking and listening, reading and writing. A benign interest on its own is not sufficient to sustain progress, there being no substitute for expert guidance from an engaged and active adult.

Engaging with artists, craftworkers and designers

Children love looking at images of all kinds, especially those in books. Adults who feel they know little about 'real' art and artists will usually confidently talk about illustrations, linking the written words with the pictures. Extending shared discussion to include comments about the way something has been drawn gives value to the image beyond its content. Comparing illustrations in different versions of the same story can open up sophisticated analysis of the style of work and what that might tell us about the artist and his or her intentions. In the same way that children might recount a familiar story, they could also draw their own illustrations discovering that the process of creating a picture is similar to the layers and sequence of a story. With the help of an adult, they can begin to see that books serve different purposes and come in a range of forms, rather like pictures.

Children can also be helped to appreciate that art takes many forms by being helped to notice images and artefacts around them, in shops, museums, galleries, homes, schools or in the media. Adams points out that in our highly visual world, visual literacy has become arguably as important as its verbal counterpart and as such will 'help children to engage with the contemporary word on its and their terms' (2001: 2). Being observant and curious are largely learned skills, developed through practice and appropriate teaching. Ruskin believed that the act of drawing taught people how to see and formed the foundation for visual thinking. If this is so, then a richly resourced environment for drawing, with ample opportunities for making a range of drawings, will support that notion. In looking at the work of artists children will see that drawings may be made on a range of scales for a variety of purposes and in a range of materials such as pencils, crayons, pens, chalks, wire, torn paper and clay.

The learning environment

Some practitioners in this country have studied the approach to learning developed in the Reggio Emilia schools established at the end of the Second World War in Italy and have attempted to incorporate some of its principles into their own practice. The schools are internationally renowned for their focus on the child's need to learn through rich multi-sensory approaches and speaking, playing, writing, painting, constructing and drawing are seen as central, related activities. The range of ways in which children communicate are known as the 'hundred languages of children', a description made famous by the touring exhibition of the same name (Malaguzzi 1993). The learning environment itself is regarded as another teacher and the wealth of graphic materials gives children opportunities to explain or express thoughts and ideas. Art is distinctive in that it is not regarded as a subject but 'an inseparable, integral part of the whole cognitive/symbolic expression involved in the process of learning' (Hendrick 1997: 21). Drawing is seen as a graphic language to be used freely in exploring ideas, describing events and expressing feelings. A striking feature of the school environment is the richness of the drawings made by the children. Visual training is an important part of every project and children are supported as they work by adults who discuss their work and help with skills. The Reggio Emilia approach to adult–child interactions is one of intense sensitivity where time is made available for children and other adults to develop relationships, skills and creative ideas and to make sense of their shared environment. It is this unhurried, unpressurised but highly skilled approach that enables children to access a wide range of complex language forms and results in 'a fluid, generative dynamic curriculum that emerges as the interests and concerns of children and adults develop together' (Hendrick 1997: 47). It also results in children making drawings of extraordinary quality. It may be that our own education system's emphasis on a restricted range of formal language systems may in reality make their mastery more difficult.

Conclusion

In this chapter we have seen the importance of understanding the nature of drawing as part of a complex language system. Children will benefit most when adults support and guide them from a position of knowledge and understanding of children's development and can then devise appropriate activities for enjoyment and learning. Activities should be planned in a rich visual environment, which matches a child's physical, cognitive, emotional, social, and cultural needs as closely as possible. Once understood, these principles can be applied in any setting. Drawing is too powerful a force in our lives to relegate to time filling. Children need to experience the pleasure afforded by the marks made by a soft pastel sweeping across textured paper or of making an intricate observational drawing of a tiny insect in order to understand and describe its qualities and structure. A drawing of a journey to playgroup can accompany that same narrative using the spoken or written word. These language systems taken together form a supporting network of communication, perception, interpretation and exploration, which enable children to develop into multiliterate, well-rounded members of society. As adults engaged with the early years, it is our clear responsibility to ensure that we provide every opportunity for them to do so.

Our tendency to think of language as primarily a form of verbal communication, and literacy as the ability to use and read language effectively in written form, does society a disservice. The current focus within education on the acquisition of numeracy and literacy need not lead to the virtual exclusion of many other important areas of learning if we adopt a multiliterate approach to our work with children, where the language systems of the spoken and written word, drawing, gesture and sound support and enhance learning development (Allen and Chisholm 2001). The concept of multiliteracy reaches far beyond the early years, enriching the lives of individuals and enabling society to benefit from the 'many ways of knowing' described by Edwards (1992: 34). Drawing can then thrive and evolve as a powerful, living language to be acquired over a lifetime.

CHAPTER 6

Developing thinking skills through scientific and mathematical experiences in the early years

Jane Devereux

Introduction

> Focussing on thinking skills in the classroom is important because it supports
> active cognitive processing which makes for better learning. . . . Standards can
> only be raised when attention is directed not only to what is to be learned but
> on how children learn and how teachers intervene to achieve this.
>
> (McGuinness 1999: 5)

> Close observation of young children at play suggests that they find out about
> the world in the same way as scientists explore new phenomena and test new
> ideas.
>
> (Roden 1999: 130)

Roden (1999) is not the first to voice these thoughts about how young children find
out about the world around them but the focus on play voiced above provides the
key to ways of extending and challenging children's learning. And as McGuinness
(1999) suggests, understanding how children learn is vital if we are to maximise
their achievements. Nathan Isaacs (1958) highlighted early scientific trends in
young children specifically:

> children's natural curiosity and interest in finding out about things, partly by
> asking questions as to what they are, where they come from, what they are made
> of, how they work and so on; but partly, also, if given the chance, by exploring
> and finding out for themselves. Secondly, their particular interest in grounds and
> reasons and above all explanations, as expressed in their persistent why questions.
> (1958: 1)

Nathan Isaacs provides insight into the nature of young children learning and developing their scientific and mathematical understanding of the world around them

that is crucial to us as early years practitioners. The aim of this chapter is to explore in more detail the implications of his observations and how they might be translated into practice in early years settings. After exploring through two case studies the 'scientific' way young children investigate and make sense of their world, time will be spent discussing the implications of this for practitioners. To do this it is necessary to look at the provision practitioners make, our own understandings of mathematics and science subject matter, as well as the processes involved in working scientifically and mathematically. The final section will explore some of the understandings and skills needed to support children's learning in these areas. The particular skill of asking questions and encouraging children to think about their own thinking (meta-cognition) and learning will be the core of this section.

Case studies

The two opening quotes set the scene for the way this chapter will examine the way children explore and make sense of their environment. Below are two case studies, one of which has a mathematical focus and the other is science based.

Case study 1: A story of one child's interest in the moon

I was driving home one October evening, with my four-year-old daughter, Laura, strapped in her car seat in the back of the car, having collected her from the childminder. She was singing 'Twinkle, Twinkle little star' to me. She had been singing nursery rhymes when I collected her. Suddenly she stopped and said the moon was moving. I asked her what she meant. The conversation that followed went something like this;

L: The moon is jumping from side to side.
M: Do you mean the moon in the song?
L: No. No. The moon in the night.
M: Is it jumping all the time?
L: Yes, it changes sides. Look it's done it again! It's on the other side now. It's your side Can't you see it? Look! Look!
L: Oh it's gone – it's hiding behind the shop. It's coming out. Quick. Look, Mum, it's back again. Hello moon!
M: I can see it. I see the moon. The moon sees me.
We were driving through an estate at the time and I was making frequent left and right turns to cut through to another main road. At the next junction I said:
M: Look where the moon is now, over the shop (to our right) and look where it is when I turn the corner. Look now. Where is it?
I turn left.
L: It's behind us. It's jumped into the back window.
I turn right.
L: No it's back on the other side. See it's moving.

Being a scientist, I try to explain to Laura in simple terms that it is us that are moving and not the moon but as you might expect she doesn't think much of my answer. So we continue to drive home and she comments regularly on the perceived movements of the moon. This fascination with the moon moving became a frequent activity on the way home for several weeks and I encouraged her to tell me where it would 'jump' to next. Laura still insisted that it was the moon that moved.

One evening, when not under pressure to get home and when the traffic was not so busy, I took her for a ride round a rectangular block of roads. Stopping at each junction before and after we had turned, I asked her to tell me where the moon was and where it would be after turning. We repeated the exercise several times. By the end Laura was able to predict which window she would see the moon in after each turn. So although not having convinced her that it was us that moved, she developed the skill to predict the position of the moon.

The change in her thinking about the moon moving came much later. One evening, I showed her that as we parked the car and I reversed onto the drive the moon remained over the house opposite even though as we moved backwards it could be seen in the side and then the front window. For Laura this seemed to be significant. As we climbed out of the car she looked at the moon, turned sideways, saying it should be on her left side and it was. Turning herself round and round, she predicted which side the moon would be on, by waving her hand. We had been playing a game about left and right for some months every time we put on shoes and Laura was quite confident about her left and right. Several days of this play followed and Laura was beginning to say regularly that it was us moving. However, for some time after this episode she continued to talk of the moon jumping, especially when we were driving around. She was more confident about us moving when we backed into the drive. She felt happy with these two ideas and was able to live with their apparent antagonism.

The difficult concept of how the earth, moon and sun move around each other was not one that I would have planned to explore with a child of this age but Laura was fascinated by the moon 'jumping' . Her ideas could have been ignored until much later in her formal science teaching but I felt it was possible to help Laura think about what was happening. At no time did I have any intention or expectation that she would reach a full understanding of the whole phenomena. It was not until much later, and many more experiences, that she developed real understanding of how the sun, moon and earth interact. Even to this day she remembers exploring the moon's 'jumping'.

This scenario raises many questions about the nature of science, the teaching and learning of science and the role and expertise of the teacher. Similar concerns could be raised about mathematics.

Case study 2: Playing a game with dice

Three nursery children, all aged 3½, were playing a game outside using a large dice and a snail spiral with boxes drawn on the tarmac (see Figure 6.1). The children

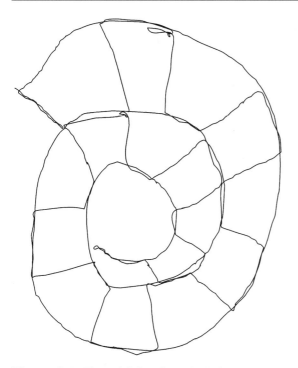

Figure 6.1 The children's spiral drawn on the playground

were throwing the dice and then hopping the same number of spots as shown on the dice. Each time the children started from the outer box of the spiral. On the wall at the side was a tally chart that the children had set up for themselves. On it they were recording each of their scores with the dice. There was no perceived order or pattern to their recording. This process of making a record was a very important part of the game and much counting and checking took place after each person's turn before it was added to the sheet. The children were able, sometimes through discussion, but often by recognising their writing, to determine which were their scores in the jumble on the page. One child was able to write some numbers and two had made tally marks. Much of the discussion about the score related to who had the most sixes and this was dependent on them being able to ascertain whose score was whose.

Next day, Annette, a practitioner who had been observing the children at intervals over several days, put up a piece of paper with three columns on the wall next to the children's chart. On arrival the three children went straight to the snail spiral and were intrigued as to why the paper was there. They put up a clean sheet of paper for themselves and prepared to play throwing the dice and calling for a six. Annette joined the children and asked if she could play and what she had to do. They explained their rules and she took her turn. When she had jumped the three steps corresponding to her dice she went to put her number on the chart. She put her name at the top of one of the columns and then drew a line across all three columns and under her name wrote the number three. The children asked what she had done and she explained that she had made a chart so that she could keep all her scores together. She also suggested that the children could have a column each to do the same and they would find it easy to see their scores. All three children were keen to do this. They wrote their names in turn and it didn't take long for them to realise they needed another column, if Annette was to play as well. The page they had put up was suggested as the fourth column by one of the children and moved accordingly. The last child wrote her name on this sheet. When another child wanted to join the game, the three children said they couldn't because there was no room to write their scores. Annette suggested that they could divide the large sheet of paper up like the other and encouraged one of the children to do it. The game then continued.

Being scientific/mathematical

The children in both case studies show a natural curiosity in their surroundings and commitment to find out and make sense of what they see. In so doing they have engaged in the processes of hypothesising, investigating, exploring and testing ideas that are crucial when working mathematically or scientifically. As she explored the moon's movement Laura raised questions, attempted to answer some herself, tested some of her ideas and sought help. She searched for patterns and was supported in her quest by a significant other, able to ask appropriate questions at appropriate times and not just for the sake of asking questions.

Children are able, as Laura shows, to hold in their head, parallel or alternative ideas. Sometimes, as Harlen suggests, 'children may hold on to earlier ideas even though contrary evidence is available because they have no access to an alternative view that makes sense to them' (2000: 54). This is how children often appear to muddle ideas and make what seem to be unrelated connections. Laura's struggle with the moon 'jumping' is an example of her keeping more than one idea in her head and selectively choosing the bits that best fit her experience of the phenomena. Her persistence and willingness to revisit and retest the same ideas show the kind of struggle that children will undertake to make sense of what they see. Her half-formed ideas are an expression of reasoning, even if not scientific reasoning, and as such should be taken seriously by adults. Children are attempting to make sense of their world, having had much less experience of the world than we have and so it is not surprising that they do not always form a complete picture first time around. Through the process skills of science children gain experience, gather evidence and see things that challenge their understanding.

Crucial to any learning experiences is children's natural curiosity of the world and their ability to stop and think about what is happening. In devising their own recording system, the children in the case study playing with the dice recognised the need to make marks to correspond to the number on the dice but they were not able at that time, except with the help of the adult, to develop their system. They may have come to the system by themselves but the role of the practitioner is to judge when and what questions should or should not be asked at different stages and times. If Annette had left the children to themselves, they may not have developed their understanding of tables for some time. The way in which Annette interacted with the children enabled them to make clearer comparisons about their individual scores and explore any patterns that emerged.

Both case studies provide signposts to the processes that support children's learning and their learning about how to learn. Both mathematical and scientific educators would recognise the process skills of hypothesising, testing, investigating, exploring, seeking patterns and making sense of their findings as working scientifically. Roden suggests that although 'young children may not be able to verbalise ideas forming in their heads . . . [they] may still apply similar processes to that of scientists' (1999: 130).

But young children do not always work in a systematic way, which is often associated with the way the public expects scientists to work, but may include much trial and error in their explorations as they try out ideas. Often, only after much trial and error and free play with objects and phenomena, are they able to predict what might happen next and to identify possible patterns emerging from their interactions. In the game with dice the children were struggling to find patterns in their scores. Even very 'scientific' scientists indulge in trial and error, as they play and test new ideas, before they develop more rigorous testing of their hypothesis. Implicit in the way scientists work is 'the having of wonderful ideas' (Duckworth 1987) and to do this there must be much thinking and connecting of experiences to wonder 'what would happen if'. If young children are to develop their scientific and mathematical thinking, they need experiences that will allow them to play with ideas and make these connections. It is important for early years practitioners to provide the kind of environment that facilitates such play and supports learning. Annette helped the children to make connections within the context of their game but she did not take over their game but played with them and their rules. The children were still in charge of their learning, accepting and rejecting Annette's ideas as they saw fit.

One of the key principles of early years education is that young children learn best through play and this contributes much to helping children learn about themselves as thinkers and learners. As Bennett *et al.* state:

Play acts as an integrating mechanism which enables children to draw on past experiences, represent them in different ways, make connections, explore possibilities and create a sense of meaning. It integrates cognitive processes and skills which assist learning. Some of these develop spontaneously, others have to be learnt consciously in order to make learning more efficient. We would like all children to become successful learners. (1997: 6)

Provision for play and learning

It is important that children feel valued, secure and confident to take risks, if learning is to be maximised. Providing a stimulating and challenging but safe environment is vital. A wide range of resources are needed to provide the breadth of experience necessary for children to be able to develop their knowledge and understanding of the world and their mathematical expertise. To support learning in science it is important that children have access to a range of materials and have the chance to manipulate such materials in different ways in order to understand the nature of their properties. This should include both the outdoor and indoor environments, thus enabling children to meet similar ideas in different settings and on bigger or smaller scales. Keeping and looking after living things will help children understand about the living processes and more about ourselves.

As children play, it is important as adults to observe what is going on and the directions the children's play and interests are taking, so that practitioner interactions with the children do not take them down unwelcome routes. Annette spent some time watching the play with dice and established their key concern as the recording of results to make comparisons. Her subsequent interventions, both in terms of resources and talk, were sensitive to the children and formed part of the play. As Hughes (1986) has noted, children can operate at much higher levels if they are working or playing in contexts that make sense. Simply putting up a table would not have helped the children begin to understand the possibilities of tables. Annette introduced some of these by constructing with the children in their play, a table that could be extended.

Providing opportunities for children to explore shape and number can be achieved in many playful ways within the nursery or other setting. Provisions such as bicycles, digging, sand and water trays, role play areas, block play, climbing frames and swings, painting, cooking, information and communications technology (ICT) and other manipulative materials all present opportunities to develop mathematical understanding and skills in contexts that are meaningful to the children. Developing a routeway for the bikes, trailers and prams can be a very constructive way to help children explore spatial concepts such as direction and distance. Pedalling bikes or pushing prams are obvious ways to begin to explore children's ideas about forces. The use of words such as 'push' and 'pull', 'harder' and 'easier', 'stronger' and 'weaker', are examples of the kind of scientific language that could be developed from playing taxis. Directional words such as straight and twisting, right and left, north and south are examples of mathematical ideas to come out of such play. It is important to explore the different understandings that children have of different words. Many of us are able to use words in appropriate contexts but if asked, cannot always explain what the word means or the scientific or mathematical concept behind the word. This is very true for many people's understanding of science with such concepts such as energy, force, density, growth and particles – all part of the big ideas of science. Ask many adults to explain density and many half-formed ideas will emerge. Many adults, as Pound (1999) acknowledges, have unhappy memories of their own mathematical experiences at school as well as science. It is vital therefore that we offer strong positive role models for children to encourage their learning. Gifford (1995) emphasises the importance of building children's self-esteem and confidence in mathematics if we want them to be successful mathematically. Providing opportunities for children to talk about their ideas, to listen to other children's ideas and to explain their thinking are crucial if we want to foster their intellectual growth.

It is therefore crucial that those working with young children have a grasp of these key and basic ideas of science and mathematics. If this understanding is linked to insights into recent research into young children learning mathematics and science, then there is a firm basis to support children's thinking and learning

Thinking skills

Other crucial factors in children's learning are the importance of the child taking the lead in the quest for skills and knowledge. According to Ball (1994), children who are allowed to think for themselves are more likely to act independently.

In both case studies the children had been the instigators of the investigations and had set the parameters for playing with their ideas. Costello suggests that 'fostering children's thinking requires more than simply imparting a requisite list of skills and strategies: the cultivation of appropriate dispositions is also of vital importance' (2000: 4).

As early years practitioners it is important to be aware of the kinds of practice and effective strategies that will encourage children to learn about how they learn.

Rath (1986) suggests that learners who act without thinking about what they are doing and those who need or seek help at each step are less likely to be successful.

Other factors that could inhibit learners making progress and developing their thinking skills include the inability to make cause and effect links, difficulty in understanding the task, lack of confidence and working within very rigid and narrow parameters. Actively working to sustain and nurture children's natural curiosity should be a priority. Providing a wide range of resources and open-ended experiences for children is important. As practitioners, we must be aware of these dimensions and develop ways and means of challenging, supporting and extending children's skills. Our aim should be to develop confident learners who have a high self-esteem and are able to take calculated risks to test out new ideas. To do this we need to listen to children, help them to consider options, give them space to try out ideas, work alongside them if necessary, provide a scaffold if necessary and help to make links.

As Rath (1986) suggests, practitioners who simply agree or disagree, or just demonstrate and explain and who interrupt children, will not extend children's ability to think for themselves. The inappropriate use of reproof rather than praise by a practitioner can reduce the self-esteem of the learner and shake the learner's confidence in the value of new ideas.

To develop thinking it is important that practitioners examine the way they interact with children and the way they set up the environment they provide. Providing open access to most areas of provision sends positive messages to children about how much you value their competence in selecting and using all the facilities and resources. It is important for practitioners to accept that they are also learners, receptive to new ideas and to the ways children work. It is crucial that they understand how they as practitioners use mathematics in their daily lives and so can see and understand why children make the connections they do. Examining the way we use questions and questioning in our daily contact with children can be very illuminating. Teachers often assume their role is to 'teach' and to do that you ask lots of questions. But the kind of questioning can give very different messages to the intended purpose. The use of questions to recall ideas and information often predominate in classrooms and often close down thinking rather than opening up. The use of questions such as:

What will happen if you . . . ? Have you thought about . . . ?
What is your problem? How can you find out about . . . ?
What happens when you test . . . ? Why do you think this will happen?
How can you fix this? What do you notice about these numbers?

all provide much more scope for the learner to explore their ideas and may help to direct their thinking and observations. The message that is sent to the learner is that you are interested in their ideas and that you are there to help them towards an answer that they have found out for themselves. In a classic work, Elstgeest (1985) lists the following five types of question as productive as opposed to unproductive:

- attention-seeking questions
- measuring and counting questions
- comparison questions
- action questions
- problem-posing questions.

He goes on to suggest that each of these types of question serves different purposes by nudging children to take more notice, to observe quantitatively, to make comparisons, to order data, to encourage exploration and to test ideas. Many practitioners often see, implicit in these types of question, the assumption that you should question children constantly but this is not the case. Children need time to think as much as adults and may need time and space to work on their own. Anning and Edwards (1999) suggest that early years practitioners have a wider understanding of their role in helping children learn and the part questioning plays in this task. Early years practitioners supporting learning in science and mathematics watch what children do and judge what they know and can do. From this they plan appropriate resources and experiences that will stimulate and challenge them as learners. The selective use of the appropriate type of question by practitioners working with and alongside children is a key requisite to developing and sustaining children's curiosity. Questions are useful to explore children's ideas about matters, because as Siraj-Blatchford and Macleod-Bradnell suggest, children's perspectives are not only different from ours 'from a physical point of view but also from a perspective developed from greater experience' (1999: 14).

The questions used by Annette to explore the group's focus for their game helped her to explore their understanding and to provide resources and support them as they attempted to solve their own problems and develop their ideas and understanding. The questioning of Laura showed that by listening to what children are saying and taking an interest in their concerns it is possible to develop learners who are confident. These learners are able to ask questions and to live with partly formed ideas as they seek further understanding or evidence to change their minds.

In summarising the essential skills needed by practitioners working with young children it is important not to forget to see ourselves as learners alongside the children. Our role is to explore their ideas, find out about their interests and how they learn and then plan appropriate experiences. As well as trying to extend children's understanding, it is necessary to develop their process skills such as observing, questioning, investigating and testing their ideas. If these skills are not developed alongside the knowledge, then the depth of their understanding will be limited. Practitioners therefore need sound knowledge and understanding of each subject area and the process skills involved. Understanding how to reflect on their own learning enables practitioners to support children by modelling and teaching a range of strategies that will allow the children to analyse their thinking and understand new ideas and experiences. Confident learners are able to take risks and learn from all experiences even those that do not always turn out as we expected. Thinking about thinking from a very early stage is vital for all learners.

CHAPTER 7

Researching young children

John Oates

'Research' – a loaded word! A word with a wealth of connotations, both positive and negative. On the positive side, what does it mean for you as an early years practitioner? Perhaps it suggests intelligent, thoughtful, progressive activity, something that will enrich your day-to-day work with children, or maybe you think more about outcomes such as gaining new knowledge or being more confident about the benefits of a new way of doing things with children. On the negative side, perhaps it resonates with detachment, coldness, even maybe a sort of ruthlessness. If this negative image dominates, perhaps you feel that research is something that other people do, and it is not for you. Or, as far as activities are concerned, it could be that what comes to mind is an image of someone who is researching a topic that seems impenetrably complicated but is also so specialised and narrow that it has little relevance to the actual issues that arise in everyday involvement with children.

In a way, both of these aspects can be true of research into children's experiences, behaviour, learning and development. In this chapter I am going to explore how 'being a researcher' in the field of early years care and education can involve taking a particular sort of attitude towards the world, which opens up possibilities for positive change, not necessarily just in a narrow professional area, but also more broadly in one's life in general. Basically, I will argue that taking a 'research' attitude involves cultivating an open mind; a recognition that one does not know all there is to know and that 'finding out' is an enjoyable and productive process.

Making meanings

Human minds have developed powerful capacities to impose meaning on the world. This is an automatic process and it goes on at an unconscious level all of the time, with us rarely needing to reflect on it. Developing a 'finding-out' attitude can be seen as quelling this impulse and instead allowing the world to 'impose meaning on us'. This takes us straight to the heart of one of the critical debates about knowledge, about what it consists of and how it might be an outcome of research, which has been rumbling around for years. In the 'people sciences' like psychology and education, which deal, basically and in large part, with relations between people, this is a central issue, since so much of what people (to use a cliché, children are people too!) do is intimately tied up with the sense that they make of the social situation that they are in. As a researcher, I inevitably find myself positioned in this debate, but I hope that I am broad-minded enough to be able to highlight some of the valuable aspects of the opposing sides in the debate. The debate is about whether there is indeed any structure 'out there' in the world, which exists independently of our making sense of it, or whether all knowledge (at least of social processes) is wholly to do with our meaning-making abilities. So, for example, is the idea of 'self-esteem' in children something that in some sense is 'in' children, or is it something that gets used as a theme in conversations in which children talk about themselves with researchers or in the way that they answer questionnaire items? In other words, is the idea of self-concept something that has been *constructed* in social interactions?

Social construction

This side of the debate is held by researchers who take a *social constructionist* (Gergen 1985) perspective, believing that most if not all of all of our experience has a profoundly social origin, that it is constructed by social interactions. For them, it is human 'meaning-making' that is all-pervasive, and they reject the idea of an independent, verifiable reality beyond our social constructions. The word 'social' is crucial here: the social constructionist view is of knowledge generation as something that goes on between people and is situated in social practices. Researchers with this orientation tend to be most interested in collecting rich data like video recordings and interview material, and their approach is to examine and interpret these materials in some depth, to gain a better understanding of the ways in which their participants make sense of their experiences in the topic area that is being researched. (The word 'participant' is now generally preferred to the term 'subject' for people who are being studied in a research project. This reflects the greater attention now paid to the significance of the relationship between a researcher and their sources of data.) Assertions of cause and effect are not often made within this style of research, but associations are often highlighted. An important aspect of this style of research when used to study young children is that it allows their voices to be heard and this facilitates their ways of making sense of their experiences being better understood. It is easy to forget that children usually see the world very differently to adults, and it takes an especially skilled approach to be able to establish the sort of rapport in which children feel able to talk freely. Where this sort of talk takes place is often especially important to children, so the choice of location must be made with care.

Positivism

At the other side of the debate, we find researchers who are often described as '*positivists*', or '*empiricists*' (Harré 1986). Their stance is based on a belief that there *is* structure in the world, including the social world, and that the task of research is to uncover this pre-existing structure. They strongly identify with 'the scientific method' as a means (perhaps the only means) of gathering knowledge, that is of things and processes quite outside and independent of our social processes. They tend to see little difference between the sort of social research that is involved in studying young children and the sort of research that studies rocks, weather patterns or biological processes, for example. This type of researcher sees social behaviour as subject to 'natural laws' which are there to be discovered and identified. The way participants talk about the research topic, the meanings that they associate with it, are not often of great interest to this type of researcher.

Qualitative and quantitative research

Researchers close to the first pole are likely to be described as *qualitative* researchers. That is, they are concerned with the qualities of behaviour and experience and, in particular, with how people talk about what is going on in the settings that are being studied. In contrast, researchers closer to the positivist pole are usually more concerned with applying *quantitative* methods. They tend to be more interested in counting up instances of behaviour or measuring aspects of what is going on in the settings of interest. For example, given a research topic such as emotional tone in home corner play, a qualitative researcher might want to spend some time watching and absorbing the quality of play and then asking the children about it, whereas a quantitative researcher might start by defining a set of behaviours that show emotional content, then using a checklist to work out the proportion of positive behaviours to negative behaviours.

A place for each research style

You may feel that you can identify more with one of these approaches than another. Rather than seeing one as 'better', though, it is possible to see them as mutually complementary, each with its own strengths and weaknesses, and each with a part to play in research. My rather stark picture of 'two camps' does not truly reflect the way that some researchers work. A quantitative approach is often useful when a researcher reaches the point of having a very clear theory and prediction(s) that can be tested for their general applicability. Often, a good test of a theory is an experiment, and quantitative methods are generally a major part of experimental studies. But reaching a point of having a clear theory also often depends on having been much less focused earlier on, and it is in these early stages of defining and refining a research topic and question that a more qualitative approach is especially useful. So each approach has a part to play in the research process. To return to the example of home corner play, a qualitative approach might well be best at an early stage, to get a feel for the processes going on and begin to develop some categories of emotionally toned behaviour. Once this has been done, it might be appropriate to move to a more quantitative position and do some counting of behaviours.

This is all rather abstract, so, to further clarify the points I am making, I am going to refer throughout this chapter to an imaginary, but I hope rather typical, example of the development of a piece of research.

Choosing a research topic

An early years practitioner, let's call her Helen, has read a newspaper article about a new, non-competitive playtime game for young children called Mill Wheel which, it is claimed, helps children to 'learn how to co-operate'. Since Helen finds that she spends a lot of her time trying to encourage co-operative work between children, she wonders whether this claim is justified and decides that she would like to find out.

Comment

Helen has cleared one of the first hurdles in planning a research project. She has a reasonably clear idea of the topic that she wants to research! She also has already got an open mind, in that she recognises that she does not know whether the claim is justified. She does not just take it on trust. So it will be relatively easy for her to formulate her research question, the next step.

Formulating a research question

This may sound relatively easy, even trivial, but the best research comes out of well-formulated questions, so your question does need some thinking about. The process of writing down your question helps you to think more clearly about it. Having a written record of what you want to find an answer to can be really helpful in keeping you on track and not getting diverted along the way. Formulating your question can also help you cut the task down to size. We all tend to start off with really big questions, that could take a lifetime or more to answer, so defining a question that stands a chance of being answered within the time that you have available is important! Discussing your question with colleagues, perhaps with other researchers, can often be a useful way of clarifying it and getting a broader perspective on it.

Helen's research question

Helen starts by writing down the question 'Does non-competitive play improve children's ability to work co-operatively with others?' When she has done this and discusses it with a colleague, she realises that this is a very 'big' question. Does it refer to any type of non-competitive play (because she already knows of several different games that are not competitive)? Does it refer to any sort of co-operative work? Her colleague points out that co-operating in home corner play is very different to co-operating in a craft activity. She is still interested in the new game, Mill Wheel, so she narrows her question down to 'Does playing Mill Wheel lead to improved co-operation in joint creative, craft activities?' She feels a bit sorry at having lost the global nature of her earlier question, but she also now realises how vague her starting point was.

Comment

Helen has already made some very useful progress in making her research question answerable, but she doesn't yet realise that there is still a long way to go in designing her study. Nor does she yet realise that this question is going to need further refinement and development.

Using Web-based resources

Research has been transformed by the new ways of accessing resources that are now available on the Web. One of the things that it is really helpful to do early on in a research study is to find out what other people have already done in the area you are interested in. You may find that someone has already answered your question for example! But more often you will find that other people have done similar things, and you can benefit from the work that they have done by avoiding pitfalls that they fell into, or you can make use of or adapt techniques that they used. Looking at other people's research reports is also a valuable way of getting further references to follow up. Depending on the sort of access you have, you can search bibliographic catalogues by keywords and download electronic copies of journal articles. If you do not have your own access to such facilities, you local library will be able to tell you what is available to you in your area.

Helen's Web search

Helen puts the words 'non-competitive games co-operation' into her Web search engine and she gets 560 hits. The first one is a website at Birmingham University which has a lengthy list of non-competitive games, links to other sites including the Woodcraft Folk, which Helen has heard about and wants to follow up, and also references to some books that look interesting. The other hits give lots of further information about non-competitive games, but not much about research in the area. Adding the word 'research' to the search does not throw up much more of relevance, so Helen logs on to the BIDS International Bibliography of the Social Sciences (IBSS) search facility www.bids.ac.uk. She still does not find any references to her specific question, in spite of varying the keywords she uses to search with, but she does find a journal article when she uses 'children & co-operation' as her search terms, that appears from the abstract to have used a standardised way of analysing videotapes of children working together. It also seems to cover some of the theory of co-operative activity. Helen is able to get electronic access to the journal, so she downloads a copy for detailed study. She finds that the word 'collaboration' seems to be used more than 'co-operation', and goes back to searching with this word. This is now much more productive, and she finds more references to both research articles and theoretical ideas.

Comment

It is worth spending some time varying the keywords that you search with, and where you search, as well as covering at least the past 20 years or so of records, to try to make sure that if something has been published on the area in which you are interested then you have found it. This sort of search often reveals interesting pieces of research that may not bear directly on the question you want to answer, but may nevertheless suggest ways in which you might tackle it.

The 'Literature Search'

If you write up your research, you will need to show that you have made an effort to find out what has already been done in the area, and that you have taken account of it in your planning and carrying out the work. This is commonly written up in a section headed 'literature search'. Writing up the results of your search is often a really useful way of further clarifying your thoughts and moving your research question on. Doing this is a good way of leading up to the clear statement of the research question and giving some theoretical backing to it.

Designing the study

This is a challenging part of research. Done well, it helps to ensure that you get results that you can have faith in; done badly, or hastily, it can lead to you finding out too late that you have overlooked something really important. If you aim to do qualitative research, the decisions that you are faced with at this stage tend to be somewhat less extensive than if you plan to do something more quantitative. Because it is not possible within the scope of this chapter to go into a lot of detail about the different types of research design, there are suggested readings at the end of the chapter that you can follow up for this sort of information.

Experiment or observation?

An early decision in designing a study is whether it will be an *experimental* design or an *observational* design.

Experimental designs

In an experimental design, the experimenter introduces some sort of change and the effects of this are monitored. The aim is to find out whether this *treatment* (the change) has an effect on some *outcome* (the effects of the change). At the same time, the researcher tries to *control* other factors that might affect the outcome, to avoid the possibility that effects due to other factors are confused with effects caused by the treatment.

Observational designs

In an observational design, there is no change introduced by the researcher; they simply study 'things as they are'. It is still an issue, in an observational design, as to whether some degree of control is needed, for the same reasons as in experimental designs. It is important also to realise that *observational designs* are not the same as *observation methods*. Observation methods, that is, watching and recording behaviour, are widely used in early years research, and I will be making some points about them later. They can be used in both experimental and observational studies, which is a bit confusing! The key point is that observational studies do not involve the researcher changing something to see what happens; if that is done, then the study is by definition an experimental one.

Helen's research design

Helen's starting point in designing her study is that she plans to introduce the play-time game as a regular feature in the setting where she works. She also plans to observe whether there are any resulting changes in the amount of what she is now calling 'collaboration' in children's interactions during craft work (which is a regular feature of the curriculum in her class).

Comment

Helen's research is now clearly developing as an experimental study, since she is introducing a change to see what effect it has. An observational study might, in contrast, examine two different settings to see whether, if one had more co-operative games, this setting also had higher levels of collaboration among children. Although Helen may not have fully thought it through, she may have tended towards her choice to conduct an experiment because she is aware that there might be all sorts of other explanations for an association arising in this latter type of study. For example, the observed differences might be due to differences in the general 'ethos' towards competition vs collaboration in the two settings, or different social backgrounds of the children concerned.

Establishing cause and effect

One of the big problems with observational studies is that it is very difficult to know whether any associations that are found are really due to direct cause–effect links. So many factors can and do influence children's behaviour and development that it is virtually impossible to control for all of these. That is why the experimental method is often seen as providing much more conclusive findings. It is important to give a lot of thought to the different factors that may impact on the outcomes that you are interested in, not just so that you can consider controlling for them, but also because this is effectively part of your own theory building.

The 'Hawthorne effect'

But, and it is a big but, there is a problem that bedevils both types of studies, particularly where children are concerned, and it is to do with the so-called 'Hawthorne effect'. It is that people's (especially children's) behaviour is very prone to changing simply because it is being studied. This effect is called the Hawthorne effect because of a study carried out in the Hawthorne electrical factory in America, that was investigating the effects of lighting and other factors on productivity (Franke and Kaul 1978). The researchers increased the level of lighting, and productivity rose. Then they reduced the level of lighting, and productivity rose again! Although more detailed analysis of the data showed that staffing changes had also contributed to these effects, the key point is that the very fact of being studied can bring about changes in the behaviour of interest. This is sometimes also called *experimenter effect*. In a way it is similar to placebo effects in drug trials, where tablets with no active ingredients may still seem to improve people's conditions. In the case of drug trials, it is clearly essential to be able to separate out such effects from the direct ones that are of interest. The procedures that are used in testing drugs are worth outlining, because the principles behind them do have implications for 'people' research more generally. The most stringent form of drug testing is the aptly named *double-blind* trial. Not only are the participants blind to the *treatment condition* (drug or placebo) that they are in (i.e. they do not know which they are being given), but also the clinicians administering the treatment are blind to the condition for each participant. It is the reasons for these controls that are of relevance to us. They recognise that people are likely to be affected by their knowledge that something is being done to them, as well as by the actual treatment itself. Any changes that occur with the placebo group give an indication of the size of this effect, so that any changes over and above this in the drug treatment group could then be attributed to true drug effects. Similarly, these controls recognise that outcomes may be affected, even unconsciously, by the people actually administering the treatment behaving differently towards the participants in the different conditions. In the case of children, the likelihood is high that they will respond to the simple fact of being studied in some way. The double-blind method is another example of an experimental control, which seeks to eliminate (or estimate) the effects of *confounding variables* on the outcomes being studied. While it is usually impossible to meet all the stringent conditions of double-blind trials in early years research, it is still worth thinking about the effects that they seek to overcome, and to think about other ways of achieving the same ends. Although these considerations are obviously important for quantitative studies, they are of no less importance for qualitative studies, where there is at least an equal risk of misleading or biased findings being gained as a result of these sorts of confounds.

Refining the design

Helen has carefully read the Methods section of one of the research papers she tracked down in her search, and realises that she needs to try to find some way of reducing possible confounding effects on the children's behaviour, that might otherwise be mistaken for real effects. She decides that one way of achieving this might be to follow changes in collaborative behaviour over a number of weeks after the introduction of the new game, since she presumes that experimenter effects might be more short-lived. She also realises that she is going to need to study the amount of collaboration between children *before* the intervention, so that she can pick up any changes.

Comment

Can you see any problems with this approach? Helen has gone some way towards removing a possible problem, but perhaps she could end up concluding that the new game doesn't make a difference if she only finds short-term changes and attributes them to experimenter effects. She would then be making what is often called a *Type 2 error*, which occurs when a real effect is not recognised. A *Type 1 error* is when a researcher believes that they have found an effect when there really is not one.

The sample

A crucial decision, for any research, is the nature of your *sample population*. Most people hope that their research will show something that has applicability beyond the specific participants with whom they gather their data, so it is important to choose a group of participants that are reasonably *representative* of the population to whom you hope your results will apply. So, for example, you would not want to just study girls if you wanted to make general statements about children's co-operation, so you might choose to have an equal number of boys and girls in the sample. Besides gender, there are likely to be other factors you might want to take into account in your sampling. *Sample size* is also an important consideration. The more different features of people that you want to represent in your sample, the bigger it needs to be. There are no hard and fast rules about how big a sample you need to have for a study; it is often a mixture of practical and methodological con-siderations that leads to the final decision. But one important factor is to do with the expected *effect size*. If the effect you are looking for is a small one, then you will need to have a large number of cases to accumulate enough evidence for it to be convincing (statistically significant, if you are using statistical analysis). This is another respect in which searching for examples of other pieces of research in your topic area can be useful; they can help you to estimate the likely effect size and hence better estimate the sample size that you need.

Helen's sample

Helen was originally thinking of introducing the new game for all the children in her setting, but just looking at changes in her own group. After having looked at other pieces of research, she thinks that perhaps her sample is going to be too small, so she raises the question at a staff meeting of other members of staff looking at collaborative behaviour in their groups, too. There is an enthusiastic response, but people ask Helen how she is going to assess the amount of collaboration, and she realises that she hadn't really thought that through at all. She had just thought that she would gain an impression of whether there is more collaboration after the intervention than before, but now she becomes aware that something more systematic might be needed.

Comment

Helen has found out another useful process in research: talking through her ideas with other people. Simply explaining what you are thinking of doing to someone else can help to highlight things that need further thought, as well as being a potentially useful source of further ideas. One of the key points for Helen that came out of this particular discussion was the need to think more about how she is going to assess the amount of collaboration in children's interactions and that simply gaining impressions is not likely to be a very reliable measure of change.

Measures

An important step in research design is the selection of the *measures* that are going to be used. This term, measure, is a very general one. It simply refers to those things that one records as descriptors of the aspects of interest in the research. A measure could be a subjective impression of the 'emotional tone' of a group, or it could be a rather precise measurement of what proportion of time two children spend in joint activity. However you choose to measure the things that you are interested in, there is always the crucial question of how valid your measures are. One of the things that is generally seen as a hallmark of useful research is that the results can be relied on, that they are valid. There are several aspects to making valid measurements. One is whether your measure is *reliable* and gives the same results, no matter where or by whom it is used. Often, being very clear in specifying how something is measured is all that is needed, so that different people can consistently apply it. This is often called giving an *operational definition* of a measure. The *reliability* of a measure can be assessed in a number of different ways, but a common one is for two people to independently measure the same thing and check that their measurements agree; this gives an estimate of so-called *inter-observer reliability*. This is a valuable technique for qualitative as well as quantitative research. In qualitative research there is a related approach that is often used, called *triangulation*. This draws on the metaphor of map-making, where a point can be fixed precisely if two people take bearings from two different triangulation (trig) points that are a known distance apart. Qualitative triangulation means getting at least one other person's perspective on the phenomenon being studied, besides your own. In early years research, this might usefully include gathering children's perspectives as well as yours. For more quantitative measures, where children's behaviour is being studied, it is often useful to make video recordings so that they can be analysed by two different people to assess the reliability of the measures. Doing this early on in a research study often has other benefits as well. For example, another pair of eyes may see things that you were unaware of, suggesting other features that might be relevant to measure.

Helen's pilot study

When Helen talks to one of her colleagues who volunteered to measure collaboration in her group, they each agree to video record five minutes of a craft session and to analyse each other's tapes as well as their own. This turns out to be very easy to do, and they realise that it has the added benefit of getting the children used to being video recorded. They spend a very interesting hour looking at these two tapes and get to the point where they have an agreed way of coding when collaboration is happening, so they can work out what proportion of the time is spent in collaborative interaction. But they also realise how time-consuming analysing video can be!

Comment

This highlights the great benefits of carrying out a *pilot study*. Trying out your measures, discussing this with someone else and refining your methods are all best done in a dry run before you commit to your main study. Helen now can feel much more confident about how she approaches the main piece of research. But there is one more thing that Helen really needs to think about. She has now gathered some video records of a number of children and recorded some analyses of their behaviour. This is privileged information and she needs to think about the ethical considerations of this. She also needs to think more broadly about the ethics of what she is planning to do in her main study.

Ethics

Recent years have seen much more attention being paid to the ethics of research than previously. Not only have issues such as the protection of identity and personal information, and the avoidance of harm to participants been highlighted, but also wider questions have been raised about the value of social research needing to be balanced by the demands made on those participating. Research on people that is carried out by, or associated with, higher education establishments is now almost universally subject to approval by some form of ethics committee. Similarly, any research that involves people and health services is subject to approval by Local Research Ethics Committees, operating within national guidelines. A number of professional associations have produced guidelines for ethical conduct in research, and for early years research, it would be appropriate to refer to the British Educational Research Association Ethical Guidelines (available on the Web www.bera.ac.uk/guidelines). Another useful source is the British Psychological Society's Code of Conduct and Ethical Guidelines (also available on the Web www.bps.org.uk). Children do form a vulnerable group, and their rights need to be protected. There are also specific issues of consent in relation to children. Ethical research practice now includes the drawing up of an ethical protocol, which out-lines the research, its procedures and resulting records, along with the procedures that will be followed for gaining informed consent and storing personal data securely. This latter point includes the need to register under the Data Protection Act any project that involves stored personal data. As far as informed consent is con-cerned, parents need to be given information about any research that is being done, in everyday terms and at a sufficient level of detail for them to be able to give consent on the basis of a good understanding of what the research entails. If you are working with children, a useful principle is that of 'assent' rather than consent. This means being sensitive to the different ways (by their non-verbal behaviour, for example) in which children can show whether or not they are comfortable with what is going on.

Ethical scrutiny

If you are not linking your research with an institution that has an ethical commit-tee, a discussion with the head of your setting about ethical issues and how you are going to approach them would be a good way to proceed, based on a written proto-col. It would probably also be valuable to seek another source of scrutiny as well, for example, by a school governor.

Helen's research

After drawing up a protocol and discussing the ethical issues with the Head of her school and a governor, Helen gains informed consent from the parents of the chil-dren who are going to participate and she carries out her study, along with her col-league. They find that the video recording goes well, and when they come to analyse the results, that there does indeed seem to have been an increase in collaborative work. But they are not convinced that this is entirely due to the new game, since the increase is much bigger for some children than others. Together, they decide to talk with the children about collaboration and they find that, in the children's talk, the key thing for them is who they are working with. Some children say that they 'weren't friends with' the other child with whom they were working and that's why they didn't want to 'let them join in'. Going back through the tapes, Helen and her colleague realise that this may be at least as important an effect as the introduction of the new game. They agree that they have learnt a lot, and that they now feel much confident about introducing the new game as a regular part of the curriculum, but they also decide that 'more research is needed' (all good research reports end with that!) and they plan another study. But that's another story.

Comment
This example, of Helen's research, shows how the qualitative and quantitative approaches both have a role to play in research, and how keeping an open mind about method as well as about the topic area is one of the keys to success.

Conclusion

Within the space of one short chapter, it has been difficult to give a comprehensive coverage of all the issues involved in doing early years research, let alone give guidance on how they might all be best tackled. What I have set out to do is to highlight some of the more important considerations, and to give, with the help of the 'Helen' example, some indications of how to proceed in developing a research design that is likely to be successful for you.

One of the most important aspects is being able to have this 'open-minded' stance, which allows you at every stage to be receptive to new ideas and new ways of thinking about your research question. Another aspect of this is being flexible and prepared to modify and develop your question so that it becomes clearer, but also easier to answer. The further readings below will take you much deeper into the various areas that I have pointed to in this chapter. Good luck and 'keep an open mind'!

Further reading

Aubrey, C., David, T., Godfrey, R. and Thompson, L. (2000) *Early Childhood Educational Research: Issues in Methodology and Ethics*. London: Routledge/Falmer.
This book is particularly useful for people new to research and deals specifically with research with young children.

Banyard, P. and Grayson, A. (eds) (2000) *Introducing Psychological Research: Seventy Studies that Shape Psychology*, 2nd edn. Basingstoke: Palgrave.
This book gives many examples of a wide range of different types of research. It also defines and illustrates many technical research terms.

Breakwell, G.M., Hammond, S. and Fife-Schaw, C. (eds) (1995) *Research Methods in Psychology*. London: Sage.
This book has useful chapters on research methods, with particularly relevant material on observation, interviewing and discourse analysis.

Gomm, R. and Woods, P. (eds) (1993) *Educational Research in Action*. London: Paul Chapman Publishing.
Critical presentation and analysis of both quantitative and qualitative approaches to educational research, with useful examples.

Hammersley, M. (ed.) (1993) *Educational Research: Current Issues*. London: Paul Chapman Publishing.
Good coverage of a range of research styles both qualitative and quantitative.

Joiner, R., Littleton, K., Faulkner, D. and Miell, D. (eds) (2000) *Rethinking Collaborative Learning.* London: Free Association Press.
This reading is included in case the example in this chapter sparked an interest in children's collaboration. It is a stimulating and up-to-date treatment of the area.

MacNaughton, G., Rolfe, S.A. and Siraj-Blatchford, I. (eds) (2001) *Doing Early Childhood Research: International Perspectives on Theory and Practice.* Buckingham: Open University Press.
Very thorough coverage of all the main issues in designing and carrying out early years research, well illustrated with examples.

Martin, P. and Bateson, P. (1993) *Measuring Behaviour: An Introductory Guide.* 2nd edn. Cambridge: Cambridge University Press.
A thorough treatment of methods for observing behaviour, focusing on quantitative approaches.

PART II

Exploring issues of inclusion

Who's listening? Who's teaching? Good circumstances for the language development of young bilinguals in early years settings

Tim Parke and Rose Drury

Introduction

Children coming into school from a bilingual background have frequently been regarded as deficient in a number of ways. Bilingualism itself has traditionally been the subject of some ambivalence in the UK, with European languages being given high status, and others, such as those of the Indian sub-continent, little status if any (Hamers and Blanc 1989). In part this has been to do with the undue regard given to languages that have a written form and a literature.

Such children have above all been seen as lacking language (above all, English) as well as lacking the cultural knowledge which would, so it is thought, enable them to succeed in the English educational system. On entry to school, their performance in English is frequently less advanced than that of their monolingual peers, and they may therefore be seen as defective in this respect. Equally serious is the fact that, since it is only possible to teach and assess children on the basis of a shared language, then where teachers do not share that of the children, it is difficult either for the children to learn or the teachers to teach, which again tends to reinforce the image of deficiency.

As against this view, we would point out that many such children, on entering school are in much the same position as their peers. That is, they have travelled the same route of development: in socialisation, in concept development, and in language. Their mother tongue may have progressed to the same level, stage for stage, as that of their English-speaking peers, and their cognitive development may also be on a par. The difficulty is that, in settings where English is virtually the only language operating, these competences may not be recognised. This produces two related problems. Where children enter an environment in which their familiar, home language is not available, they are unlikely to use it: nobody speaks a language if no response is likely to be forthcoming. Second, when such children do begin on the development of English as their additional language, there may be little dedicated attention and support to further its progress.

In the present chapter, we take up the topic of bilingualism in early years settings in order to examine two main issues. The first is the extent to which children have the opportunity to develop a high level of language, in relation to the expectations of the educational system, parents and others. The other is the extent of adult intervention in the child's language, beyond the talk generated between the child and her peers. In order to look at these issues, we have examined in detail transcripts of a child in her nursery (see below for details of the data collection), and analysed them in two complementary ways. One is by examining the grammatical features of the language, comparing them with monolingual norms, and thus assessing that aspect of her competence. The other is by examining the functions of language (Halliday 1975), i.e. what the child shows evidence of being able to *do* with language.

Following our analyses of the data, we raise the fundamental question of how the kind of language interaction we see generated in early years settings, both between children and between children and adults, is likely to favour the language development of the child concerned. We ask whether:

- language is sufficiently directed to the level the child has attained;
- there are opportunities to acquire and rehearse new terms;
- adults ever focus closely on language;
- adults ever seek to increase the demands made on the child. (cf. Tarone and Liu 1995)

A third, less prominent issue that we will develop from this data is the nature of language policy in early years settings, as compared with guidance given in the QCA's *Curriculum Guidance for the Foundation Stage* (QCA 2000).

Our data are part of a wider study of three bilingual children learning in early years settings and at home (Parke and Drury 2001). Nazma, Samia and Maria (not their real names) were studied during their first year of formal education in three multi-ethnic nurseries in Watford. The families of all three girls originate from the Khotli area of Azad Kashmir, which borders North-East Pakistan, and their mother tongue is Pahari (a dialect of Punjabi spoken in this area).

In this chapter we focus on one of the three girls – Maria. The detailed focus is her English language development as observed in a given setting (see the transcribed data, below), but we consider first her early socialisation at home and some of the 'starting points' for her learning as she enters the schooling system. We then go on to look at her experiences in the early years setting.

Maria at home: starting points

Maria is the eldest child of two in her family. She lives with her extended family: two sets of grandparents (who live next door to each other), parents, cousins, aunts, uncles and her younger brother. Two of her aunts went to school in Watford and her uncles are still at school and doing well. The family has lived in Watford for seven years. Maria's father lived in Pakistan as a boy and arrived in England as a teenager. He did not attend school, but attended evening classes to learn English. He now works in a factory in North Watford, a town about 35km north-west of London.

Maria understands Urdu but does not speak it. Her father used to speak Urdu to her when she was younger, but she now speaks Pahari to her grandparents, parents and younger cousins and sibling. All the children are fluent in Pahari. Her aunts and uncles use English in the home and Maria tries to join in. Her mother comments: 'She is fine – she tries to speak any language.' She does not yet attend Qu'ranic classes, but her mother says that she imitates the adults, covering her head and trying to read the Qu'ran. Maria did not attend playgroup; her early socialisation was in the home playing with her cousins and younger brother. Her mother comments that she 'is happy playing by herself and with her cousins and her little brother at home. She tries to be the leader as she is the elder sister. She sings songs in Pahari and plays in her own little world.'

There were strong links with Pakistan in Maria's early years. She had a six-month stay with her family before starting nursery and her father visits Pakistan regularly.

A nursery school perspective

Maria started nursery when she was four years old and spent three terms there. Her nursery teacher and two nursery nurses are nursery practitioners who have considerable experience of working with bilingual children and their families. During an interview in the first few weeks of her first term, her nursery teacher viewed her as confident, and 'brighter than other bilingual children – I knew she was going to achieve'. However, the nursery nurse noted on her Nursery Progress record for Term 1: 'Maria was cross with everyone for being left at nursery in the early days and cried every day.'

Her Nursery Baseline Assessment scores underlined the challenges faced by Maria and staff during her early days at nursery. She scored 20 out of a possible score of 41, with significant areas for development in *Language Experience/Mathematical Experience* (she scored 3 out of 12) and *Approaches to Learning* (she scored 4 out of 9). Maria was, however, seen by her nursery teacher as coming from a loving home which nurtured confidence and had high expectations of her: 'her strong personality will get her through. She is quick to catch on'. Her Nursery Progress report for the second half of the first term reflected this view: 'Maria has shown herself to be a very determined and intelligent girl, tackling all aspects of nursery with enthusiasm and skill (providing she has chosen the task).'

In relation to her language development, her nursery teacher observed that Maria loved stories and is keen to bring her book bag in to nursery. Her teacher commented that Maria was keen to learn English and the staff supported her by 'talking to her a lot', adding that the bilingual classroom assistant works with her twice a week. She considered that Maria would 'go from strength to strength' in the future.

Early days at nursery

The vignette presented below is based on observations made of Maria during one session in her fifth week at the nursery.

Maria enters nursery and finds her place on the carpet alongside the other 28 children in the class. This is her fifth week. She had cried during her first days, but she is quiet now. At the beginning of the morning the teacher introduces the activities for the session to the whole class. It is then small group time and Maria joins a nursery nurse for a planning session. In response to the question repeated three times 'Maria, what would you like to do?', Maria replies 'painting', and moves over to the hand-painting activity table. She paints alongside Kiran silently and then washes her hands. She then moves to the dough table and sits with two English-speaking girls who are engaged in imaginative play, making cakes. Maria is silent except for one interaction. When one of them asks 'Can I have some more cake?' she responds emphatically 'No'. At the cutting activity Maria is making a face using paper shapes and a nursery nurse interacts with her. She makes one-word responses to questions about her face: 'one', 'two', 'nose', 'mouth', 'eye', 'brown'. Maria moves over to the carpet and plays with wheeled toys and a small construction on her own. Then she stands and watches the other children. She sings 'ba ba black sheep' to herself quietly as she plays. It is home time and she is collected by her Auntie at the nursery door.

In this vignette of Maria during her first few weeks at nursery, the following points can be made:

- She is at an early stage of English language development; she uses one-word utterances when questioned by the nursery nurse.
- She has already learnt the routines and procedures of the nursery and she is able to participate in activities without speaking to other children; she plays quietly on her own for much of the time.
- There is no evidence of use of mother tongue in the nursery (except when a bilingual classroom assistant is present).

We now consider a transcript of Maria during her third and last term at nursery and we focus here on her English language development.

Maria at nursery: approx. one year later

This excerpt from a longer audio recording shows Maria on the carpet playing alongside two monolingual English-speaking children (Ch 1, 2, 3) with a small construction.

Maria: Coat, shoes [speaking to herself]
I want do that one
Give me this one please

Ch 2:   [indistinct]

Maria: Up you get
[singing to herself]
I can jump
I can jump
I can jump

Maria: Come on let's do that one

Ch 2:   That one's two guns
Matthew done guns
Don't do any

Maria: Come do that one
do that one
Look I do a pooh pooh

Ch 2:   Don't do any guns
What's this
Pink thing
Get out you pink thing

Maria: Go away you idiot

Ch 2:   Why did you say that
Oops a daisy

Maria: Oops a daisy

Ch 2:   Oh a pooh
Don't do them guns

Maria: I do other one let's do it I can't
I can't do this right
Can't do . . .
Do like do
Do like
Do like this
Do like this
Do like this

Ch 2:   You do that one
And you do that one
And you do that one

Maria:	Do that
Ch 2:	No I can't
Maria:	You can't
Ch 2:	Can you?
Maria:	Can't do that one
Ch 2:	I'll do this
Ch 2:	How do you make a gun with this
Maria:	Oops
Ch 2:	How do you make a gun with it
Maria:	Oops a daisy
Ch 3:	Huppsy wuppsy
Ch 2:	How do you make a gun with this
Maria:	Gun do it see [indistinct]
	Do you like this
	Do you like this

Findings 1: language forms: a first analysis of the transcript

One way in which linguists and others routinely analyse the level of attainment of children in the acquisition of language is to look at the grammatical features they have developed at a particular stage. This kind of analysis draws on very robust findings in child language research (e.g. Brown 1973) which show strongly predictable stages of development, quite closely tied in to specific ages. The caveat is that these stages are nearly always based on monolingual norms, and so, at least in so far as the age expectations are concerned, cannot be applied naïvely to bilingual children. However, the sequence of the stages is normally found to be the same for them as for monolinguals (Juan-Garau and Perez-Vidal 2001).

An analysis of the data here reveals the following features. Maria's English shows some errors that can be described as developmental. Although, as we have seen, she has a first language which has progressed to a normal level for a child of her age, she is making a small number of errors in her English. Yet these do not differ from those made by a monolingual child acquiring English as a first language. Harris's work has shown that in such situations, language acquisition proceeds along the same sequence for both languages (Harris 1992). That is to say that the *route* of acquisition of English is the same as for a monolingual child, while the *rate* of acquisition may differ. Thus her path through the English language is the same as that taken by a child acquiring English only, but, because Maria is also acquiring Pahari at the same time, and has in fact done this to a level normal for a child of her age, she has not reached the level of her monolingual peers. In effect, she is doing two things to their one.

Maria's errors are not always consistent: that is, in some cases, she has two versions of the same target (i.e. standard) form. For example, she says both 'You want big one? (not using 'do'), and 'Do you like this?' (including 'do'). Later in the exchange, she says both 'I'm making this' and 'You making rubbish': i.e. in the first case, she includes the auxiliary verb 'am', in the second she does not. It may seem that in this Maria is being inconsistent, but research has shown that for a learner to have two forms available, one correct and the other not, is a typical interim stage (Ellis 1988). So far from being a sign of uncertainty, this shows that Maria has acquired both forms, and can ultimately be expected to choose the correct one on the basis of the reinforcement she will receive from others. Another feature is Maria's past tenses, which show the influence of the dialect of the Watford area. Forms such as 'I done' are common, and will probably be the norm for her.

She uses a number of modal verbs, especially 'can'. It is worth pointing out that these verbs are usually seen as late-acquired, because they have a less obvious literal meaning than 'typical' verbs that encode actions. So it is usually thought that the verb 'kick' encodes a concept that is easier to understand than, for example, the verbs 'would' or 'shall'. We can take from this that she is making good progress in her learning, and is showing some evidence of handling sophisticated concepts.

Another issue is the extent to which Maria's English is influenced by her first language. The most noticeable way in which this might happen would be through her pronunciation, and if we were to listen to the tape of this whole interaction we would probably detect the influence of her distinctive Pahari sounds. Another source of influence could be seen in her use of auxiliary verbs and articles. These can be seen as inherent difficulties of English, i.e. as examples of where English is simply a hard language to learn, partly because these two features form a contrast with many other languages, many of which, including most Asian languages, encode these meanings in different ways. In English, using or omitting the article allows us to specify these gradations of meaning (see Table 8.1). Other languages express these distinctions using different methods, and a learner used to one way takes time to adjust to expressing them using different means.

One striking feature of the full transcript is that Maria has acquired a very wide range of imperatives, ranging from suitably rude to markedly polite, and uses them appropriately. They are set out in Table 8.2.

Finally, Maria does not use a form such as 'There's a blue one' (the so-called 'existential' form), but says 'Blue one there' instead. It may be that she does not yet have this former structure in her repertoire: in this, she is again following the normal developmental path, the word 'there' being used first by children to mean a place, and only subsequently in constructions of the type 'There's a blue one' in which 'there' has no specific meaning.

Findings 2: an analysis of language functions in the transcript

Looking at grammatical development is only one way of looking at language. An equally important way is to examine exactly what the child is doing with the language she has at her disposal. Rather than looking at form, we can look at function: rather than look at what the language *is*, we can look at what it *does*.

Table 8.1   Ways of referring to the definite and indefinite objects

Head	Example
Car	Car is the most popular means of transport
Cars	Cars are a nuisance and should be banned
The cars	The cars were parked in a row
The car	The car I saw last week has disappeared
A car	A car passed in silence

Table 8.2   The range of Maria's language strategies for influencing others' behaviour

Imperative	Occurrence
Let my do it	1
Let my show you	1
Get off	1
You off that	1
You come down	1
Look, I cut this	1
Give me this one please	1
Let's do that one, Let's do it	1
Come do that one	1
Go away you idiot	1
Do like [this]	5
Do that	1

In her class, Maria interacts successfully: she fills the role of a schoolchild participating in group work. She completes her task to the satisfaction of the nursery nurse. She holds her own with her peers: specifically, she negotiates, assesses her own behaviour, makes offers, elicits opinions, criticises others, and directs others (see Table 8.3).

In this context, Maria spends most of her time interacting with her peers, and deploys, as we have noted, a wide range of language functions. She is operating here at her own level. The tasks – writing her name, cutting paper, playing with floor puzzles and working with dough – focus on physical, here-and-now activities. To a degree, language is additional: it adds a means of communication between co-operating children. It has, as we have seen, the roles of negotiation, offering, and so on. So this 'child-generated language', that is, language that the children generate without adult intervention, is helpful to the successful running of the task, in terms of going through the activity in this particular situation.

Table 8.3 Language functions in Maria's discourse

Function	Example
Negotiate	Give me this one please
Assess own behaviour	Can't do that one
Make a suggestion	Come on let's do that one
Elicit opinion	Do you like this?
Criticise others	You can't roll and you can't put
Direct others	Go away you idiot

We can also consider the language generated by the adults present: the teacher, a nursery nurse, and a bilingual classroom assistant (BCA). Their role, as presented in these extracts, is to comment ('That's very nice', 'It looks like samosa'), to suggest ('Can you cut your caterpillar?'), to direct ('Children in my group, if you would like to go outside . . .', 'You should be tidying up'), and to check behaviour ('Are you in there? Who's that?'). There is a single case, in the adult–child exchanges, where Maria appears to express a more personal meaning: where she stands back from the activity she has been carrying out, and is thus given an opportunity to start to conceptualise it. It comes when she rejects the construction the BCA puts on her actions:

BCA: What's this? [in Pahari]
Maria: Chicken.
BCA: Chicken.
         It looks like samosa.
Maria: I'm making chutney, not sausage.

In this brief exchange, Maria produces the most complex language evidenced in the whole transcript.

Discussion

The focus of this discussion is the actual and potential levels of the language demands made on Maria in this setting. To what extent does her language remain at a level that facilitates other activities, and to what extent does it become a focus in itself?

We have suggested that, at least in so far as the transcript presented here goes, language can be categorised simply as either child- or adult-generated. Child-generated language occurs naturally between peers, in the course of acts of negotiating, offering, eliciting opinions and criticising. According to Halliday, it has an inter-personal function (1975); it is of itself virtually a form of social action, having as much of a social role as, say, passing a toy to another child or giving up one's place at the dough table. This is not to say that it is insignificant, but only that its function is closely related to the personal dealings that children have with one another. A characteristic of it is that language itself does not have a specific focus: it is, to its users, purely a means to an end. It is, as most language is, embedded in the activities which give rise to it; it is unself-conscious.

The point is equally true of the adult-generated language. We have characterised the functions of the adults language in the transcript under discussion as commenting on the results of an activity, suggesting a new move in an activity, and directing and checking children's group behaviour. Just as much as the children's, this language emerges naturally from the activity of early years settings: it is largely the language of management. While it is concerned with (the children's) behaviour, it is itself embedded in that behaviour, and is not directed at enabling the children to stand back from their activities and see them for what they are. We suggest that this only happens on one occasion, 'the chutney/sausage' exchange, in which Maria rejects the interpretation the BCA has put on her activity.

The question we raise is the extent to which such language should be left at the level it attains in interactions between children. An explicit aim of nursery education is to promote young children's language development. On the one hand, it can be argued that language that derives from activities that are themselves natural and well designed for young children is almost bound to do this. It is claimed that linguistic development is motivated by the need to express personal meanings, and, if there is a 'rich environment' – i.e. a lot of talk going on around a child – development is inevitable. It is the kind of thinking Bourne characterises when, reviewing the mechanisms by which bilingual children have been subsumed into mainstream classrooms, she says:

> The development of children's languages could be seen and dismissed as something which could be left to be acquired 'naturally', where children heard the languages around them at home and in the community; it would not require planned teaching interventions. (Bourne 2001: 261)

Two points can be put to counter the view that it is enough for the child to have access to language to develop it fully. One is that, while there may be a lot of language going on around a child, this does not inevitably mean that there will be uptake from it. It has sometimes been thought that simple exposure to language is enough to guarantee acquisition, but it is obvious that, for example, face-to-face conversation, directed specifically at a child, sensitive to the child's known interests and language level, offers somewhat more possibilities for learning (Mercer 1995). Mere exposure is also not likely to be sufficient in cases where a child coming to an early years setting has little experience of the predominant language she will find there (Parke 1993).

This is exactly Maria's case. She has grown up, as we have seen, in a largely Pahari-speaking environment, in a family who see it as their role to develop and nurture their first language and culture. We know that her Pahari was at a typical level for a child of her age on entry to early years settings: that is, she has experienced a normal language development. Although she has had some accidental, unsystematic and unsustained exposure to English simply by dint of living in the UK, her nursery is the first monolingually English environment she will have experienced. One of her tasks now is to tune in to a relatively new language, which will incur a level of adjustment to new sounds, words and usage; in fact, a partial reanalysis of what language is. While it is clear that her English is developing normally, exhibiting only the slight lag that is typical of bilinguals (Cummins 1984), we should also consider what is being done to develop and extend it. A prime concern of her current language development is for her to add to her existing home language competence the second layer of language skills that will help achieve success at school. For example, close attention to her listening and speaking activities could lead to, first, an analysis of the vocabulary she lacks in English. Analysis of the errors she is currently making could allow a comparison of these with those of other bilingual children from similar language backgrounds, and so to more focused teaching. There can be a danger that errors, if left unnoticed and unresolved, become fossilised and embedded in the learner's normal repertoire.

The second point is that language does not develop to its highest potential if it is left to itself. There is no evidence to suggest that the best way for a young potential bilingual to acquire English is by neglect. Language does not develop in the way educators, parents and even governments want and expect it to if left to itself. There are implications here for the approach to language to be taken by early years settings.

Finally, the issue of language policy. It is almost obligatory for an early years setting to proclaim a multi-lingual policy in its documentation, and to state there that the use of the mother tongue is welcomed. How this operates in practice is very variable. It may be that an early years settings will vigorously promote a mother tongue policy, employ BCAs, encourage child – child and adult – child interaction in the mother tongues their children enjoy, have the resources to sustain them, and celebrate them as living witnesses of other cultures. It is equally possible that settings have a tacit policy of English-only, acting under an impulse to have all children speaking English fluently in readiness for school (baseline assessments).

Conclusion: implications for practice

From the issues raised in this chapter, we can highlight three implications for early years practice. First, activities need to be designed to include opportunities for the development of language. At the very least, if language development is not an explicit aim of the activity, early years practitioners can ask 'What kind of language will naturally emerge from this activity? Can the language be extended and built on? Who will be available to monitor what the bilingual children say, and can we make use of their recorded samples for future planning?'

Second, activities should be planned bearing in mind opportunities for children to have purposeful interactions with adults. Occasions for bilingual children to have prolonged, focused and structured dialogues with adults in early years settings are precious.

Finally – although this is a larger issue on which we have only touched here – bilingual staff, or other bilingual adults, should spend time on an agreed planned basis using mother tongue for routine interactions. What their mother tongue can do for them need not be identical for all young bilinguals, but it is potentially the vital source of a child's linguistic, cognitive and social development, and as such is a critical resource.

CHAPTER 9

Parent partnership and inclusion in the early years

Alice Paige-Smith

Introduction

In this chapter I consider different perspectives towards parents of children with learning difficulties and disabilities and how the concept of parent partnership has developed. An analysis of policy documents which describe parent partnership indicates that there has been a shift in perspective from a 'supportive' model in the 1970s towards a 'rights' model represented in the Special Educational Needs Code of Practice (DfES 2001b). Parents are considered to have the right to participate in their child's education and to indicate their choices in their child's schooling. Local Education Authorities are instructed in the Code to provide parents with independent advisors to support them in making these choices. This shift will be outlined in this chapter by considering the conflicting attitudes between parents and professionals and how one particular group of parents supported and became involved in the education of their children in the early years.

Parents and professionals

Since the 1981 Education Act there has been a repositioning of 'special educational needs' in the early years within an inclusive framework (Wolfendale 2000). Issues of inclusion in the early years were first of all recognised in the Green Paper *Excellence for All Children*, Meeting Special Educational Needs (DfEE 1997b) and the subsequent Programme of Action (DfEE 1998b) announced initiatives such as Sure Start (Wolfendale 2000). Alongside these developments there has been a growth in expertise for practitioners working in the early years with children who experience difficulties in learning or have disabilities (ibid.). The notion of 'parent partnership' in the early years has also been recognised in the *Curriculum Guidance for the Foundation Stage* (QCA 2000).

The 1981 Education Act represented a major change in the education of children; the term 'special educational needs' replaced previous categories of learning difficulties that had been based on assessments by professionals. The term 'special educational needs', which could be considered to be a label which replaced previous ways of categorising children, came out of discussions during the Warnock Committee in 1978. This Committee recognised that 20 per cent of all children would experience difficulties at some time during their school career. The Committee also recognised that input from parents was important during the assessment process. A statement of special educational needs was recommended by the Warnock Report (DES 1978) as a way of assessing a child's needs and provision, and in 1981 parents were given the legal right to participate in this process. Approximately 2 per cent of children have statements of their special educational needs.

However, while the 1978 Warnock Report had a chapter dedicated to parent partnership, this could be considered to have a patronising attitude towards parents. Professionals are considered to be the people who know or are the 'experts' on the child. This theme recurs throughout the education of children with learning difficulties and disabilities and the notion of parent partnership has developed as a way of recognising the tensions which exist between parents and professionals. An example of the attitudes towards parents is in this extract from the Warnock Report:

> Parents must be assisted to understand their child's difficulties. They must also be helped to adopt attitudes to him most conducive to his feeling that he is accepted and has the same status in the family as any brothers or sisters. (Department of Education and Science 1978: Section 7.19)

Parents are considered to need help in order to understand and accept their child. Models of how parents 'parent' their child who has a disability or learning difficulty have been proposed by professionals (Mittler and Mittler 1982; Cunningham and Davis 1985). These may neglect the difference in the power relationship between parents and professionals and also the relationship with the child. Chris Goodey, the parent of a child with Down's Syndrome, has written about parental attitudes, based on a study of parents of children with Down's Syndrome (Goodey 1991).

Professionals and prejudicial attitudes

Incidences of prejudicial attitudes towards disability and difficulties of learning abound in the literature on parents' experiences. Professional practice may fail to consider the best interests of the child where his or her opinions differ from those of the parents. Doctors have been criticised for the way they break the news to the parent that they have a disabled child because they pre-judge the child: 'When my son was two he was diagnosed at a London hospital. I [the father] saw the doctor. He just told me that my son was an imbecile, then closed the interview by ringing for the next patient' (Furneaux 1988: 9). The parents of this child were told by a paediatrician to 'put him away and forget you ever had him' (ibid. 1988). These parents found the doctor's judgement painful to experience. They did not perceive their child in the same way as their doctor.

Birth and the early years are considered to be hard for parents especially if they have a child with a learning difficulty or a disability. They are recognised to go through stages of shock through to acceptance during the diagnosis of their child's learning difficulty or disability (Cunningham and Davis 1985). Cunningham and Davis discuss parents' reactions in their book written specifically for professionals:

> Parents may consider killing the child or leaving it in the institution. These should be seen not as mere pathological reactions to stress, but as strategies serving an important purpose . . . They are potentially beneficial and should not be discouraged. (1985: 31)

Some parents have attempted to redefine what this period of time is like for them. They stress the negative attitudes of other people towards their child, including professionals (Goodey 1992).

Parents – challenging ideologies

Challenging perceptions of disability or of difficulties of learning is an experience common to parents of children born with Trisomy 21 (so-called Down's Syndrome). Chris Goodey (1992) researched how parents' experiences clashed with the professionals' perceptions of parenting a child with Trisomy 21. Contrary to the myth that the child is automatically rejected by the parent who 'mourns the death of the normal child that didn't emerge', Goodey reports that parents feel the expectation of rejecting their child is imposed on them. Parents are subjected to ideologies of how disability is perceived, in the first instance, by professionals, like doctors, and nurses, and others, such as family members. He suggests in his research carried out with 18 families, that parents challenge perceptions of disability and difficulties of learning held by professionals in the medical field:

> Like many of the parents, Rita readily agrees with the professional maxim that 'It's natural to feel shocked', but she clearly does not take this to be some scientific and objective concomitant of the situation, something in her genes. Such parents know that it is something they have been socialised into by a segregated society, and that things could have been otherwise: that they ought to be otherwise. (ibid.: 170)

Claiming that parents become 'includers' through their experiences and contact with members of the 'excluded' group, their power to change prevailing views is negated by the institutionalised power of professionals who define and dominate practice:

> For the clinical and educational professions (and the lay notions which derive their values from them), their very practice makes it clear what fact it is that you 'come to terms' with: you have not given birth to a member of the human species as we define it, and to which we allocate certain rights and social roles, but to an

object of pathology – a 'monster', to use a technical term employed in medical anatomy. For the parent, the same phrase means the inverse: I have not given birth to the monster which my upbringing and socialisation led me to believe I'd had, but to a normal member of the human species as I now define it. (ibid.: 172)

Parents, Goodey suggests, go through a process of de-socialising themselves, and with this process emerges the realisation that perhaps the professionals are also socialised into their roles and expectations. Potentially they too can be de-socialised and find a 'common language' which is not the language of 'partnership' between 'parents' and 'professionals' as this is a false division that describes power relationships that come with roles allocated to individuals. The real division is instead manifested between the 'strange tribe' and the 'real people':

There is a strange tribe that believes in spells, psychometric assessments and incantations, and there is a tribe of what Beverley, Devon's mother, calls real people . . . They may be parents or they may only have letters after their name, but what they have in common is this: they know that intellectual perfection and the criteria for measuring it are chimeras. (ibid.: 176)

Goodey, as a parent of a child with Trisomy 21, is advocating inclusion as a belief, or a philosophy. He suggests that an inclusive philosophy may be held by parents and others who have experienced a 'shift in human values'. This may have occurred because these people have been directly exposed to the way society and professionals reject the humanity of disability. In a 'segregated society' disabled people and people with difficulties of learning are excluded, isolated, rejected, treated as problems and as not belonging to the rest of society. They can work in sheltered workshops, live in group homes or institutions and be educated in special schools. For Goodey, segregation boils down to a question of rival philosophies of how disability and learning difficulty are perceived in society and education. He states that parents can share the same perspective as each other, as can professionals, but this involves taking a leap across from one paradigm to another. 'There may be differing views of what "humanity" consists of behind it all' (ibid.: 166):

Philosophies clash and compete. As far as those who experience difficulties in learning or have disabilities are concerned there are 'excluders' and 'includers'. The excluders, since theirs is the prevailing view in our educational and other institutions, want to keep convincing the world at large that their choice as to who belongs is the only possible one. This necessitates them saying something about the rival philosophy of the includers in addition to conveying the appearance of expertise (ibid.: 166)

The ideology of a segregated society according to Abberley (1987) 'devalues impaired modes of being, at the same time as it naturalises the causes of impairment' and has supported the historical developments of institutionalised ways of categorising people.

Parents' experiences and views – ensuring inclusion

What are parents' experiences if they have a child with learning difficulties or disabilities?: what are their experiences in the early years?: how do these relate to their involvement in education and their choice of inclusion? Robina Mallet set up a parents group in the West of England to support parents and provide information for them, she has articulated what it is like to be a parent – she could be considered to be a 'professional parent' as she provides advice, information and support for other parents:

> The title a professional acquires gives status, recognition of the body of knowledge they have achieved and perhaps reinforces self-confidence. The social standing of a parent of a child with 'special needs' seems to depend to an extent, on the disability experienced. This can range between 'super human' to 'ineffectual parent'. Wherever the judgement rests we may be perceived uncomfortably – other parents feeling sorry for us or suspecting we resent their 'better fortunes'. We are (accidentally one hopes) frequently called 'special needs parents'! (Mallett 1997: 29)

Other parents have set up parents groups since the 1981 Education Act and I interviewed eight parents to find out what their experiences had been and why they had become involved in setting up parents groups (Paige-Smith 1996). The experiences of these parents indicate that they had similar philosophies and attitudes towards their children, these influenced the choice of schooling for their children. Jane's experiences illustrate the barriers in ensuring inclusion and how some of these barriers were overcome.

Jane's experiences

Jane had set up a parents' campaign and support group with other mothers whose children attended a pre-school playgroup, they wanted their children to attend mainstream schools rather than a special school which was the practice of the local education authority. When Jane's son was a year old he was diagnosed as having cerebral palsy. Jane joined a local playgroup funded by social services and MENCAP. This playgroup had been established in her town for children referred by social services because their children experienced difficulties in learning or were disabled. When all the mothers from the playgroup met they realised they had a common concern:

> We all got together one day and the biggest thing we were concerned about was education. Talking together we all found that we had a common concern about our kids – that when they reach five, where are they going to go? (Jane)

This group of parents became concerned about the practice of sending all children with disabilities or learning difficulties to special schools. Disabled children in the area could attend a special school for disabled pupils, but Jane was not satisfied with the prospect of this for her son:

If a child had spina bifida, say, or cerebral palsy, or a physical disability they would be bussed or taxied to Coventry which is the nearest school. So, for young children, often as young as four, because they often liked them to go to nursery, they would be spending up to two hours travelling. We thought that was appalling, given all the problems our kids have anyway, you know, isolation, to spend all that time travelling – and it's very expensive.

The mothers from the playgroup arranged for a parents group from Coventry to visit and talk to them. They were impressed with this group and decided to set up a campaign and support group in order to try to ensure the inclusion of their children into mainstream school:

> These parents came along from Coventry and said, 'Look we have fought for our children to go to mainstream schools.' We thought , 'Gosh, can we all be like these people, they know all these things!' We wanted to get a support group going, because there were a lot of issues, not only about education, but the statementing procedure, and the way that professionals deal with you and how you very much feel on your own. We wanted to give each other support and together we can find out as much as we needed to know, and information is power, isn't it? (Jane)

The parents became empowered when they recognised that other parents had similar demands for their children's education. Mark Vaughan from the Spastics Society (who went on to set up the Centre for Studies of Inclusive Education) talked to the parents following their visit from the Coventry parents group. Hearing from these people made Jane and the other parents realise that they needed to set up a parents group in order to reduce their isolation:

> We realised that people had worked out that they wanted integrated education, but because they are on their own, they are pressurised to send them to the local special schools. Because they hadn't had the support of the group they hadn't been able to fight for it.

Jane described how the parents group emerged out of a group of parents who shared similar views on what they wanted for their children. The group, which began with a group of mothers meeting informally, turned into a structured group with a set of aims. They gathered and disseminated information to support their campaign, they decided on a name and met every week. The group raised funds by holding jumble sales and organising conferences. The parents group invited the head teacher of their local special school along to their first conference on integration. The group felt that it was important to have a dialogue with the head teacher because Jane said that he held a different view of integration to that of the parents. The parents wanted their children to be included into mainstream school, however, they thought that the head teacher wanted their children to attend the special school and to be partially included into mainstream school for certain lessons.

Officers from the local authority were also invited to the conference but did not turn up. Subsequently, letters were written by the parents' group to the local paper about the lack of interest from the local authority. Officers responded by saying that they did not attend because they had not been individually invited to the conference. The parents' group were in dialogue with the local authority, they had lots of meetings with education officers and would attend Education Committee meetings. The parents were asking for support for their children to attend mainstream school, however, the local authority wanted the children to attend special schools:

> They were saying, ' I'm sorry but I have got no money'. I mean, it always came down to resources. They said, 'Look, the special school, is there – there is separate funding for that and for mainstream.' They didn't have a policy, the authority didn't even have a written policy, they were just hoping that they could carry on as normal. They were saying, 'We've got the set up and that is it, basically.' (Jane)

The parents group responded to the 'deadlock' situation with the local authority by providing individual support for parents by attending meetings with them to talk to education officers. The group also ensured that disabled people at open meetings provided information on disability awareness issues. As people came to talk at the meetings from different parts of England the parents recognised that inclusion varied according to location. This knowledge strengthened the aims of the group and reduced their sense of isolation:

> Once people found out if you lived in . . . [another county] . . . you were alright, you could get integration – it very much depended on which county you lived in as to what sort of service you got, so people thought, alright, we'll try and get that here, so it gave us ammunition. (Jane)

Individual parents in the group, including Jane, were pushing for their children to be integrated into their local mainstream schools, rather than segregated into the special schools in the local authority. Her son, Alexis, would have been bussed to the special school in Coventry. Instead, Jane put his name down at the nursery at the local school where her eldest son attended. However, she found the head teacher hostile to her son attending her school, and she was very concerned about the prejudicial attitudes towards her son's disability:

> The head teacher said, 'O.K., well, we'll see when the time comes.' Anyway when the time did come the letter that was sent out to welcome new parents to the nursery, I didn't have one. So I went to her and said, 'O.K., what's going on?' – she was quite frightened of us actually, and she avoided me for quite a long time, and I cornered her in the hall in the school and I got very upset about it and I drafted a letter to the governors and she wouldn't have him and I said, 'Why won't you take Alexis?' I mean it's awful when you are actually saying 'Well, he's quite a nice boy really' and all this kind of shit. You know, having to sort of persuade people to take your children to school, and she [the head teacher] said: 'Well, he'd

take up too much space, and maybe later, when he'll be walking by that time', because he had a rollator then, he wasn't walking at that time. (Jane)

The head teacher told Alexis' father that she feared she would get a flood of handicapped children in the school if she let Alexis and another disabled child in. Alexis' parents were told by an education officer that 'he wouldn't want his son in a classroom with a handicapped child in it'. These prejudicial attitudes meant that Alexis' parents were unable to trust professionals:

> They would say lots of things and then they would completely deny that they said that and so we had a policy that we would take a tape recorder in to meetings, or I would go along and take notes, and they didn't like that at all, that really got up their nose. But of course, they would say things in one breath and then say they'd never said them. I mean you couldn't trust them at all. (Jane)

The authority had an 'unwritten' policy of refusing full-time support in mainstream. Alexis was finally granted 10 hours support in mainstream because of his difficulties in reading and writing. Jane feels that his support benefited the whole class and the class teacher because she had an 'extra pair of hands'. The decision to make this support available to her son was made by an education officer. Jane thought that the authority had 'backstepped' on their decision not to provide support because of the cost of transporting her son to special school.

Jane managed to ensure that her son was integrated into his local school, however, three other parents from the group tried for three years to get their children into their local mainstream school. It proved harder for these parents because, Jane suggests, their children were categorised as having 'severe learning difficulties'. The appeal process experienced by these parents has been written about by Will Swann (1987). These parents kept their children at home for three years and fought their case collectively. However, they lost their local appeal to a panel and to the Secretary of State. Meanwhile the children were at home not receiving any education; Jane described what happened to the children and their families:

> A tragedy occurred. One of the parents died, so they dropped out of these fights and the child went to residential special school, because there was no-one to look after the children. Of course all the parents found this really disheartening, but they carried on, they are tremendous people, they have been together all the time and then there was a change in education officer and they said that if the children went to the special school for half the week they could go to mainstream for the other half. The parents . . . were so desperate, they had the children at home all this time and then both parents had to find a school that supported them. Two mainstream schools had them for a while on an experimental basis and then they said they couldn't carry on because they weren't getting help in educational assistance. They weren't getting any teaching support, the special school wouldn't give it. That was one of our arguments with them. We said, 'There is all this expertise and it's locked in there, get it out, get it into mainstream and share it around.'

While Jane managed to ensure the inclusion of her child into the local mainstream school, this was not possible for the parents of the three children categorised as having 'severe learning difficulties'. The barriers to their inclusion were the local authority's inability to provide support in mainstream for these pupils and the lack of flexibility of the special schools to provide support in mainstream for these pupils. According to Jane, the local authority had 'no morality, philosophy or commitment' to integration.

The parents from LINC continued to work through encouraging disability awareness in their local community. The group LINC were also involved in the national parents group Network '81. The two groups found that they had a common aim for parents, children and young people.

Parental involvement

Robina Mallett (1997) has written about her involvement in setting up the parents group in the West of England and the services and support that are provided for parents. Jane's experiences also illustrate how parents' collective experiences can lead to their empowerment and involvement in decision-making concerning their child's education. Major changes have occurred in the development of parents' rights since the 1981 Education Act, as the Special Educational Needs and Disability Act (2001) has recognised children's rights to attend mainstream school and parents' rights to assert this choice. The power of local education authorities, and hence professionals, to segregate children in special schools has been reduced through the changes in education law which have been campaigned for by disabled people and parents groups (Rieser, 2001).

In the *Curriculum Guidance for the Foundation Stage* (QCA 2000) there is a section on 'Parents as partners' which recognises that each setting should develop an effective partnership with parents which consists of: 'A two way flow of information, knowledge and expertise'.

Practitioners should do the following:

- show respect and understand the role of the parent;
- listen to parents' accounts of their child's development and any concerns they have;
- make parents feel welcome;
- use the knowledge and expertise of parents and other family adults to support learning;
- keep parents fully informed about the curriculum;
- talk about and record children's progress and achievements;
- extend relevant learning and play activities such as reading and sharing books, so that they continue at home. (ibid.: 9)

The guidance for children with special educational needs and disabilities also suggests that:

Early years practitioners have a key role to play in working with parents to identify learning needs and respond quickly to any area of particular difficulty, and to
develop an effective strategy to meet these needs, making good use of individual
education plans, so that later difficulties can be avoided. (ibid.: 18)

The Foundation Stage documentation does suggest that there are links between
parental involvement and the curriculum of the child. It is suggested that parents
should be informed about their child's experiences and their progress and that activities should be extended into the home. Individual Education Programmes provide
a way of recording and evaluating children's learning if they have learning difficulties or disabilities that can be shared with the parents. The documentation also recognises the value of parents' views and states that they should listen to parents.
Robina Mallett, who set up the parents group in the West of England suggested that:

Parents often are the only people who know everything that has happened to the
child. They actually carry a body of knowledge that the other professionals
haven't shared in whether they are carrying messages from the medics about diagnosis and things which just haven't been shared. It is often as if the parent is the
key worker in what is going on. Some will be able to cope with that, others can't.
What they actually know should be respected. They know that their children
need encouragement . . . they know when they get tired, they know their likes
and dislikes and how much they like being teased or joked with. (Robina Mallett)

Conclusion

The Special Educational Needs Code of Practice (DfES 2001b) does recognise this
perspective and parents are considered to hold 'key information' and to have a 'critical role to play in their children's education' (ibid.: 16). Effective communication
with parents by professionals, according to this document, should draw on parental knowledge and expertise in relation to their child. However, in the section on
key principles in communicating and working in partnership with parents, the role
of parents as participants in supporting their children's learning is not emphasised.
The section on the roles and responsibilities of schools and in particular, the Special
Educational Needs Co-ordinator notes that parents should be encouraged to participate, but that they may need 'emotional support', indicating that there may be
conflict experienced by parents (ibid.: 26). The role of local education authorities
and parent partnership has been outlined in the Code of Practice. LEAs are
instructed to provide: 'access to an independent Parental Supporter for all parents
who want one', as well as 'accurate, neutral information on their rights, roles and
responsibilities within the SEN process, and on the wide range of options that are
available for their children's education' (ibid.: 21).

The Code of Practice does acknowledge the ways in which parents should be provided with information and support in order to understand their rights and roles in
the education of their child with a learning difficulty or a disability. The 1978

Warnock Report suggested that parents should be 'helped' to adopt the right attitudes towards their child, the shift in the past 20 years has been towards a 'rights' model of parent partnership. Perhaps this shift is due to the actions of parents and parent groups that have campaigned for changes in the attitudes and perspectives of professionals.

CHAPTER 10

Including a deaf child in an early years context: issues for practitioners

Joy Jarvis

Jessica, Manjit and Katy are four-year-olds in their local nursery school. It is 10 o'clock and they are playing at the water tray. They have plastic trays and some clothes pegs. They move the pegs on the trays and drop them in the water. There is a lot of splashing and laughing. About 10 minutes later a nursery nurse joins the group and brings some jugs, beakers and bottles. She stays with the group, talking and joining in the pouring activities. Suddenly she leaves the group to see to a child who has climbed on a table. She lifts the child down from the table and he starts to cry. The nursery nurse talks to the group which has gathered round. Jessica, Manjit and Katy watch what is happening before they return to their activities. A few minutes later they pull off their aprons. One of Jessica's hearing aids slips from behind her ear in the process but she puts it back and all three girls run out into the garden.

Jessica has a severe hearing loss and is the only deaf child in her local nursery school. Deaf children have been attending mainstream early years provisions for many years and indeed about 85 per cent of deaf children now attend mainstream schools (Lynas *et al.* 1997). For at least the last 30 years the move in the UK, as in much of the rest of the world, has been away from children with special needs attending special schools and towards their placement in mainstream contexts. This is emphasised by the Code of Practice: 'the special educational needs of children will normally be met in mainstream schools or settings' (DfES 2001: 7). Including all children in mainstream provisions aims to provide equality of opportunity and is often seen as a human rights issue, particularly in the United States where separation of schools along racial lines led to inequality of provision.

Deaf children were some of the first children with special needs to be 'integrated' and to be seen as benefiting from access to mainstream provision. Looking at the scenario above it may seem clear why this might be. Like the two hearing children, Jessica had no problem using the equipment available, she could concentrate on the tasks and follow the routine of the nursery. However, concern is being expressed that deaf children are not achieving as well as their hearing peers academically (Powers *et al.* 1998) and may be more isolated and have lower self-esteem in mainstream than in special contexts (Musselman *et al.* 1996). In order to understand why this may be the case, we need to consider both the needs of the deaf child and the process of learning.

Who is the deaf child?

Hearing loss

The terms 'deaf' or 'hearing impaired' cover a range of hearing loss. Children with mild or moderate losses will hear sound at a reduced volume, will hear parts of words and will respond variably to sounds depending on the context. Those with severe or profound hearing loss will not hear speech without hearing aids and the speech that is heard will be distorted and in some cases minimal. These children will generally have either hearing aids, which are usually behind the ears with an earmould in the ear canal to channel the sound, or a cochlear implant, whereby electrodes have been inserted into the inner ear and the child has a receiver attached to his or her head by a magnet. These amplification devices do not restore normal hearing and speech will not be heard clearly. Background noise is also amplified and this can mask speech and also distress a child who may be sensitive to loud sounds. Often a child will also have a radio system for a context when he or she is in a group. In this case the speaker will have a microphone and the effect is that of the speech signal being close to the child's ear. This is important as the further away the child is from the sound, the more difficult (or impossible) it becomes to hear it and the more sound in the environment will mask speech (Tate Maltby and Knight 2000).

Language

Deaf children do not have a language problem as such, rather, they have a problem accessing enough spoken language in order to use their processing abilities to create language for themselves. They do not have a complete model of the language because they will hear a partial, distorted version of English and see, on the speaker's lips, ambiguous information (the sounds p/b/m, for example, all look the same). This will result in imperfect understanding and the production of speech which may be unclear or unintelligible, particularly in the early years when speech and language are developing. A deaf child in an early years context is likely to have comprehension and use of English that is very much delayed in relation to others of the same age.

Because for some children accessing language by ear is so difficult they will learn it by eye through British Sign Language (BSL). BSL is a complete, grammatical language so children who have access to adult models, such as deaf parents who use BSL, can learn the language at the same rate as hearing children learn a spoken language. However, the vast majority of deaf children are born to hearing parents who, if they decide to use sign language, will be learning it themselves. In this case their children will have access to an immature language or to signs in English word order (Sign Supported English). These children's communication in both sign and speech is therefore likely to be delayed when they enter early years provisions (Powers *et al.* 1998).

Issues for learning in an early years setting

The consequences of linguistic delay or difference are significant in an early years setting in which spoken language is a primary means of learning. The importance of language for children's learning in all early years contexts may not seem immediately evident. In the water tray activity described earlier, for example, the three children appeared to be undertaking the same activities and therefore could be seen as having the same learning experiences. A closer observation would show that this is not the case.

Jessica, Manjit and Katy are at the water tray. Manjit suggests that the pegs are a family; she gives them all names. The trays are boats at the seaside. She talks about her last holiday when she went on a boat. Katy says that the peg people are on the boat. She splashes the water to make the sea rough and says that the people are frightened. She drops a peg in the water saying that the baby has fallen in the sea and might drown. The other pegs are dropped in to perform a rescue. The splashing and the storm get worse.

Jessica doesn't hear what the other girls are saying. Their speech is quick and quiet, drowned out by the noise of the water and the brick play going on behind them. She drops pegs in the water and splashes.

When the nursery nurse joins the group she talks to the children about their pouring activities, she uses a range of related vocabulary: full, empty, more, less, how many, not enough. Jessica joins in the pouring activities. She looks carefully at what she is doing but she cannot look at the activity and watch the adult's face to try to lipread what is being said.

The nursery nurse goes to the boy on the table. Manjit and Katy hear her explain the dangers of walking on the table and the likely consequences. Jessica sees that the boy is crying and that the nursery nurse has a cross expression on her face.

It is clear from this closer observation of the activity that Jessica's experience is very different from the other two girls. She did not understand the representational nature of the first activity, the idea of 'pretending' something, nor how the activity in the water tray could be related to past experiences at the seaside. While the other two girls were engaged in sharing past experiences and inventing imaginary stories, Jessica was engaged in the physical experiences of dropping pegs and splashing water. To make sense of the present in the light of experience is crucial to learning and is most easily done through language. To imagine future events and to hypothesise, as well as to revisit previous experience, one needs some form of symbolism and again language is the most effective. Katy and Manjit were developing their narrative skills, supported by each other's contributions, skills that will help them to understand and express their knowledge of the world. They were also exploring the world of feelings: how would you feel if you were on a boat in a storm? Deaf children can have difficulties with the language of emotion, often being unable to express or understand what they or others are feeling as they have not had the range of opportunities to explore these (Marcschark 1993).

With the pouring activities, the two hearing girls are laying the foundations of early mathematical knowledge and language. Through language the nursery nurse was pointing out and labelling significant aspects of the activity. Through repeated, supported experiences the hearing children will come to understand concepts of conservation, comparison and quantity. Jessica will come to understand these concepts too, but later than the other children, because she lacks access to the linguistic support given by adults and peers (Wood *et al.* 1986).

When the nursery nurse was explaining the dangers inherent in table climbing Jessica was not understanding the explanation, she was only seeing the activity. Reasons, causes and explanations support children's emotional, moral and social development. While young children are often not clear why two events e.g. two broken windows can be seen quite differently (one was the result of an accident and one was deliberate) they come, through explanation and discussion, to understand motivation and moral reasoning. Without access to linguistic explanation deaf children's development may be delayed in this area (Marcschark 1993). The three girls at the water tray were not involved in the table walking situation but two of them could overhear what was happening. Gregory *et al.* (1995) argue that because deaf children are often only able to understand what is said directly to them, and are unable to overhear conversations, they miss a large proportion of the information hearing people use to learn about the world. Their knowledge of the world takes longer to acquire.

Inclusion of deaf children is more complex than it first appears. Language is central to the learning process. Adults and peers use language to scaffold and support learning and the child uses language as a tool for thinking (Bruner, 1975; Donaldson 1978; Gopnik *et al.* 1999). Any child with insufficient mastery of the language used in an early years setting will be at a disadvantage in relation to most aspects of development. Studies of deaf young children in nurseries and schools suggest that in many cases they did not have access to the curriculum or to social interaction to the same extent as their hearing peers. (Gregory and Bishop 1989; Hopwood and Gallaway 1999). One observational study of three deaf children individually included in their local nursery classes concluded: 'They had neither full access to information, nor interpersonal interactions on an equal basis' (Monkman 1995: 98). Concern has been expressed that some deaf children individually included in mainstream settings may have difficulties with social relationships and with their development of identity and self-esteem (Marcschark 2000; Nunes *et al.* 2001). Retrospective interviews with deaf young people and adults point, at times, to feelings of isolation, rejection and frustration (Gregory *et al.* 1995; Sheridan 2000).

Early years practitioners welcoming deaf children into their settings need to be aware of these issues in order to ensure that inclusion is an active not a passive process. Including a deaf child is not to do with placing a child in a particular location but with practitioners working with families and with other professionals, such as teachers of the deaf, to address issues and to seek solutions. These solutions will involve analysing learning in the particular setting in relation to the individual child. They will involve observing learning and providing appropriate support. They must involve having high expectations of what deaf children can achieve or limited achievement will be seen as acceptable (Powers *et al.* 1998).

Implications for practice: active inclusion

Active inclusion involves working with families and professionals to develop and monitor strategies. These will involve adapting the environment and the curriculum and using additional support appropriately.

Liaison with family and professionals

All early years practitioners aim to have positive relationships with the families of children in their care. Parents with children with special needs are particularly vulnerable when their child first goes to an early years context as the procedure is not as straightforward as for other children. They may feel that their child is being rejected and that this is a foretaste of what will happen in society for the rest of the child's life (Carpenter 1997). It is important that early years practitioners appreciate the emotional aspects of this transition and that parents may need additional support and understanding. Welcoming the child and identifying his or her strengths are an encouraging start.

All children need adequate preparation for entry into an early years context. Deaf children will need the same good quality preparation as other children, including visits to the child's home by practitioners. As Willey (2000) notes, this provides for developing shared knowledge and understanding of individual and family needs. Continued sharing of information can be supported by a book in which practitioners and parents can write or draw significant events. This can support the child's communication with others about what has happened. One picture of a slug in the lettuce on Daddy's plate, for example, excited tremendous interest in a group of four-year-olds when a deaf child used it to explain an event the evening before! Families of deaf children will have been visited, usually on a regular basis, by a teacher of the deaf. This teacher will liaise with the practitioners in the early years setting. Practitioners need to know what continuing support is being given to the child and if any other early years contexts are involved. Deaf children may attend small group sessions with other deaf children, for example. Ongoing liaison with the teacher of the deaf, whereby the needs of the child are identified and met, needs to be undertaken (RNID 2001).

The social/emotional environment

Deaf children need to feel part of the early years group. Many older deaf children and adults recall feeling isolated and different from other children when they entered educational contexts. Often this was because they could not see other children who used hearing aids or communicated using sign language (Sheridan 2000). They did not see themselves represented in the settings. Early years practitioners are aware of the need to show images of different racial groups and to have a range of culturally appropriate materials, regardless of whether children from different groups attend the setting. It is equally important to have positive images of children and adults with special needs, such as books with children in wheelchairs or using hearing aids as part of everyday life. It is essential for all children that differences are celebrated and not ignored. Children are aware that we are not 'all the same' and to pretend otherwise can damage the self-esteem of the deaf child who may feel that he or she is a failure in relation to hearing children (Ladd 1991).

Some deaf children will assume that they will not need hearing aids when they grow up as they do not see adults with hearing aids around them. If older deaf children and adults can spend time in the setting, this will enhance the deaf child's developing self-image. One deaf five-year-old had a visit to Father Christmas with his reception class. His excitement in discovering that Father Christmas had hearing aids was only matched by his annoyance that no one had told him this important fact before! It is important for all children, not just deaf children, to have their attention drawn to hearing aid users, in order to raise the status of this population.

The listening environment

The communication environment for the deaf child is enhanced if noise levels can be reduced. Carpet tiles, less noisy containers for equipment and blinds for windows can all help. Practitioners need to ensure that the child's hearing equipment is 'in, on and working' and parents and the teacher of the deaf can demonstrate replacing hearing aids that have fallen out of ears, or changing batteries. Other children will be interested in the equipment and it is important for the deaf child's self-esteem and acceptance that this is acknowledged and dealt with in a matter of fact way. For hearing children to be told that they are 'lucky' that they don't have to use the equipment or that 'poor Suzy' can't hear properly will not enhance the deaf child's status within the group or their own acceptance of their deafness. The aim should be to concentrate on what the child can do. One deaf parent brought a flashing light baby alarm and a vibrating alarm clock to his child's nursery class, much to the delight and admiration of all the children.

The communication environment

Communication is likely to be the biggest concern that the practitioner may have initially. Will the child understand the adults and children in the setting and will they understand the child? Getting to the child's level physically, so that the face can be seen, will help. Smiling and using a range of facial expressions and body language will aid communication as will use of gesture and visual support such as objects and pictures. Deaf children are often very skilled at getting their meaning across, even if they have very limited vocabulary, provided the environment is supportive and encouraging.

If the child has sign language as a first language it is as unrealistic for practitioners to learn BSL, as it would be for them to learn Somali or French if they had children who spoke those first languages. Learning a few important signs would be helpful, however, and the ability to understand key signs used by the child would ease frustration. It would be anticipated that a child using BSL would have a deaf, or fluent sign language user present in a supporting role but the child's teacher or key worker would also want to communicate directly with the child as much as possible. Some practitioners may have used Makaton, which is a collection of signs used to support English. It is not a sign language but may aid communication between the adult and child.

Deaf and hearing children in early years contexts may develop means of communication between themselves. It is important, however, that this is not just left to happen, as deaf children often lack experience of effective communication, including non-verbal skills. Pair and small group activities with adult support, particularly in the activities where the deaf child shows strengths, can encourage interaction. Hearing adults and children will need to appreciate that deaf children, particularly those from deaf families, will use touch for interaction more than hearing children and it is important that this is not misinterpreted as roughness. Children with limited linguistic skills may be more physical in their communication and this needs to be handled sensitively.

For children to be confident in a setting, they need to understand the routine. Visual means of explaining the sequence of the day, and of the week, as children get older, need to be used. Picture calendars showing the sequence of the day are important. So too are clear visual explanations of rules such as 'only 4 children in the play house' or when it will be the deaf child's turn to go on a bike. A hearing child will be given a verbal explanation but the deaf child may well not understand, will become frustrated and either withdraw from activities or take what they want.

The learning environment

Language development

Deaf children may be placed in early years contexts with the aim of developing their delayed language. However, group situations may not be the best contexts for this. As Tizard and Hughes (1984), Wells (1986) and others found the quality of adults' interactions with children at home is almost inevitably better than in contexts with a higher child–adult ratio and a different agenda. Even in care contexts for very young children, adults may feel constrained to use their language more for management than for supporting linguistic development (Jarvis and Lamb 2001). Following the child's interest, providing contingent utterances related to an individual's activities and modelling appropriate language may not be evident in all early years settings but are important for all children at an early stage in learning language (Wells 1986). For deaf children the situation is even more complex as the noise level in a group setting is likely to be such that it masks speech. A quiet setting for small group and individual activities, where appropriate language can be used, would be better. Interaction can include developing vocabulary for objects and activities in the setting which can be shared with the parents for generalisation at home. If the child is developing BSL, then a fluent signer would need to undertake the same activities, adapting and modifying signing input in relation to the signing abilities of the child (Harris 1992).

Group time

In most care or education contexts there will be time when the children are in a large or small group with an adult for a story, discussion or other activity. These are often fairly quiet times, when the children are focused on one adult and where there is usually an expectation that people will speak one at a time. If the deaf child can see the adult clearly this will increase the chance of understanding what is said. If the adult repeats or summarises children's contributions then the deaf child will have some access to these. Spoken language will need to be supported by pictures or other visual aids. Stories told with props are more easily understood. It is important that time is allowed for looking at the props as the child cannot look at these and lipread at the same time. Due to different language levels it is unlikely that a story read to the group will be understood by the deaf child. A supporting adult will be able to sign the story for a child using BSL but the child cannot look at the interpreter and at pictures at the same time, so the pace needs to be appropriate. If a child has shared the group book with an adult on an individual basis in the setting or at home, then the child will be able to understand and contribute more easily in the group.

Video-taped stories can be impossible to understand without access to the sound track. Often only some events are portrayed visually and reasons and explanations are given orally. The deaf child sees a number of apparently unconnected events and has no access to the reasoning behind what has happened. Again, the learning context for the deaf child is limited, leading to potential problems understanding cause and effect except at a very basic level. Some cartoons can be understood visually and are often thoroughly enjoyed by deaf children. If the deaf child is a BSL user, then taped signed stories can be shown to the group in much the same way as one would share a book with a written script from another language. This again supports the child's feeling of being accepted and belonging in the group.

Developing areas of strength

As with all children, it is important to develop deaf children's strengths. These will be individual but may include strong visual skills, an awareness of pattern and shape, the ability to complete picture puzzles quickly and an awareness of print in the environment. Deaf children may be interested in maps and plans and indeed may be skilled at identifying routes by visual cues. They may notice and be interested in numbers and may start to use these in pictures. Labels on photographs and objects may help a deaf child locate materials and matching the printed names with photographs of children in the group can help him or her to learn friends' names. Deaf children may begin developmental writing at much the same age as hearing children if others in the environment are writing and it is important that adults demonstrate the purpose and function of writing by, for example, giving instructions in print. Understanding that speech or signed communication can be written down can be helped by using speech bubbles in activities and stories.

Books for young children to read usually contain natural language so that the link can be made between spoken and written language. For deaf children, their language is likely to be different from that found in texts. Sentences in books will be longer than those the children are using and words such as 'it', 'the' and 'to' which do not appear in early speech and which are difficult to lipread will be present in print. If the deaf child is to make sense of what reading is about, then the child needs to read text at his or her own linguistic level. This may mean starting with home-made books with photos and pictures and basic texts generated by the practitioner on the computer such as 'Barbara jumping', 'John swinging', 'Peter's cup', 'big shoe', 'my drink', and so on. The teacher of the deaf would be able to identify the appropriate language level for an individual child. The appropriate choice of printed books to read is vital if deaf children are to learn that what they read can make sense. Books need to have limited and repeated vocabulary and sentence structures if they are to be understood. Again, advice would need to be sought from a teacher of the deaf.

The role of additional adult support

An education or care context may be given funding for some hours of additional adult support. For a child with BSL as his or her first language, this would usually be a fluent sign language user. For a child developing English as a first language the adult would need good communication skills, including clear speech and lip patterns. In either case the child would need sensitive support; too much could lead to the child being isolated from peers, too little would mean that the child is not gaining enough linguistic input and interaction. Monkman's (1995) detailed observation of three deaf children attending their local nursery classes found that each child interacted with their supporting adult most of the time and had minimal interaction with other adults or with other children in the setting. Practitioners need to ensure that the child is not 'swamped' by too much support and thereby not allowed to develop independence and relationships with other children; however, the child needs as far as possible to have access to the same information and language input as the other children. This balance is difficult to achieve and requires continual monitoring. In the water play scenario described earlier, Jessica's supporting adult, Pam, could have aided her understanding of what was going on without being intrusive. Pam has worked in the nursery class for four years and has undertaken a teaching assistants course. She has been involved in planning with the nursery teacher and nursery nurse in the provision. Together with the advisory teacher for the deaf, the early years team has been developing appropriate strategies for communication and supporting learning. The team is continually reflecting on practice and considering priorities for support.

Pam observes the three girls choosing their aprons for water play. They are arguing over who will have the red apron but she does not intervene. She helps another group of children organise themselves for painting. When the girls are settled at the water tray Pam observes the play until she sees that Jessica does not understand its representational nature. She joins the group and asks the girls about the pegs. She names Mummy, baby and the other pegs so that Jessica is clear that these are pretend people. Then she leaves them to carry on the game.

Pam notices the activity undertaken by the nursery nurse and notes in the home-link book the key words used. She writes these round a picture of the water tray so that Jessica can explain the activity to her parents and they can reinforce the vocabulary. She also records in Jessica's record book that this activity will need to be undertaken on an individual basis and which vocabulary needs to be used. When she has individual time with Jessica, Pam will use water play as a basis for interaction and will also use opportunities in other play activities to use the related vocabulary. At snack time she could talk about full/empty glasses, more fruit, another piece. The skill of a supporting adult is to identify the language and concepts that need to be developed and to bring them into everyday activities.

Pam sees that Jessica is watching the incident with the nursery nurse and the boy on the table. She explains to her, using mime as well as language, why the activity was dangerous and what might have happened. When the girls run out into the garden she watches from a distance but does not become involved in their chasing game. She takes a photo of the game using the new digital camera and will use this later in the day as a focus for discussion. Before Jessica goes home the photograph will be stuck in her home link book so that it can be discussed with her family.

Discussion

There is a tradition of early years practitioners welcoming all children and including them in their settings. Current legislation and guidance expect this and provide structures, such as the Code of Practice and the development of the role of Special Needs Co-ordinators, to support this practice. Inclusion of children with special needs in education and care contexts is part of a wider national agenda of developing a more inclusive, equitable society (Thomas 1997). For early years practitioners issues arise in relation to practice – what is the best way of including a particular child? This chapter suggests that practitioners need to work with families, and with professionals who have specific areas of expertise, in order to identify needs and develop appropriate strategies. Additionally, early years practitioners need to use their skills in observation to understand the process of learning in their setting and to identify when and how learning needs to be supported. The early years team in Jessica's nursery school observed and reflected on their practice and actively supported her inclusion. The also appreciated the extent to which her learning was affected by her language delay. As the nursery teacher noted: 'The trouble is, she looks the same as everyone else and you think she's learning the same as the others, but she's not.' Many included deaf children are 'invisible' in their education or care context and do not receive the support necessary to flourish. Only through an active process of observation, reflection and action can practitioners ensure that deaf children receive the quality care and education they deserve.

Useful source of information

The Forest Bookshop, Unit 2, The New Building, Ellwood Rd, Milkwall, Coleford, Glos. GL16 7LE 01594 833858 www.ForestBooks.com
This bookshop provides books on deafness, children's books and videos.

CHAPTER 11

Health inequalities in early childhood

Angela Underdown

Children who are healthy emotionally and physically have the energy and motivation to play, explore, experiment, learn and form relationships with others. A healthy childhood is not only important in its own right, it also lays the foundations for health in adult life. Jason, for example, is not experiencing the positive emotional or physical health that might be expected of a child living in a prosperous and developed country like the United Kingdom.

Jason and his mother, Jacky, have recently moved into a women's refuge to get away from Jason's father, Ned, who has become increasingly violent. Jacky has always been short of money and lately Ned has been spending most of his wages on alcohol. Jacky's depression started when she was pregnant and, although she loves Jason, she found it difficult to form a close emotional bond with him. Jason has frequent temper tantrums and has become very aggressive with other children. Jacky is finding it hard to get Jason to the new nursery since they moved and he has missed even more sessions because of chest infections. The health visitor thinks that Jason's cough would improve if he wasn't always in a smoky atmosphere and if he lost some weight. Jacky has been trying hard to cook healthy food but Jason will only eat burgers and chips.

Families in the UK are experiencing many changes, as divorce and separation rates increase and support from traditional networks decrease. In addition, three times as many families in 1998 were living in relative poverty compared to 1979 (DSS 1999a). These changes, among others, have a dramatic impact on children's emotional well-being and physical health.

This chapter takes a broad overview of the health inequalities affecting children in the UK at the beginning of the twenty-first century and evaluates how early interventions may promote better long-term health. Attention is drawn to changing patterns of health and to how poverty creates and compounds health inequalities. Recently children's health has taken a higher profile on the national policy agenda, with numerous initiatives aiming to reduce health inequalities and improve children's health. Interventions to support the health of young children are discussed, with particular focus on the Sure Start initiative, which offers an innovative partnership approach to the primary prevention of ill health from conception until the child is four years old.

Changing patterns of health in the United Kingdom

A hundred years ago, children's health was threatened by infectious diseases such as tuberculosis, polio, measles, whooping cough and diphtheria but today, these threats have been contained by improved living conditions, hygiene and immunisation. However, there is little room for complacency, as tuberculosis rates, for example, are increasing again and there are fears of measles and whooping cough epidemics when immunisation rates drop. There are new threats to children's health reflecting the changing environmental and economic circumstances. Few children in the UK are at risk of starvation, yet the rate of childhood obesity, with all the long-term emotional and physical ill effects, is soaring (BMA 1999). Accidents pose a major threat to young children's health, particularly affecting boys from poorer families. Children face danger from traffic and have less safe places to play and exercise, and the rates of asthma are increasing in most developed countries (OPCS 1995). The apparent rise in the number of children experiencing emotional and behavioural difficulties is of concern, resulting in countless children having problems making friends and maintaining relationships and underachieving at school. *Bright Futures* (1999: 6), the report from the Mental Health Foundation, describes the incidence of mental health problems:

> there are approximately 14.9 million children and young people under twenty living in the UK, representing 25% of the population. It is calculated that at any one time, 20% of children and adolescents experience psychological problems.

Thus, although the overall physical health of children in the UK is improving, this masks huge variations and the new patterns of ill health that are emerging. There are variations in health and well-being in different ethnic groups, in different social classes and between different regions of the country (BMA 1999). The government has recently published a consultation paper aimed at tackling health inequalities in the UK and in this the Minister of Health, Yvette Cooper, states:

> What greater inequity can there be to die younger and to suffer more illness throughout your life as a result of where you live, what job you do and how much your parents earned? Yet at the turn of the 21st century, opportunity for a healthy life is still linked to social circumstances and childhood poverty. (Cooper 2001: 3)

The effect of poverty on children's health

The evidence about the effect of poverty on children's health is not new. Nearly 60 years ago Titmuss (1943) emphasised the link between being brought up in a poor family and increased ill health. Yet the numbers of children being raised in families where the income level is 50 per cent or less of the average income (about £10,000 per annum in 2000) increased dramatically over the past 20 years. In 1979, 1 in 10 children lived in a household with below half the average income, but by 1999 this had risen to 1 in 3 children (DSS 1999b). This dramatic increase in children living in families with insufficient income has had a devastating effect on children's health, with the gap between health experienced between those in highest and lowest income groups becoming ever wider. Issues, such as disability, often put added financial pressures on a family. Parker (cited in BMA 1999) concluded in his study that 55 per cent of families with a disabled child were living in or on the margins of poverty. The BMA report also highlights the severe disadvantages of ethnic minority families with disabled children:

> The barrier of inadequate information and lack of interpreters, the reluctance to offer some services, such as respite care, because of misunderstandings about the role of the extended family and the poor housing and poverty exacerbate any problems of care. (1999: 103)

Many children face situations where their health is compromised, but living in a family with insufficient income frequently compounds these difficulties, as can be seen in the following overview.

Children who live in families experiencing relative poverty are:

- less likely to eat a healthy diet

People in lower socio-economic groups shop more carefully to obtain more food for their money but they are more likely to buy foods with high levels of fat and sugar because they are richer in energy and cheaper than fruit and vegetables (Leather 1996; Acheson 1998).

> Why do children from poor families consume such a lot of fizzy drinks, milk and white bread? Penny for penny, a chocolate bar provides more calories than carrots, even from a market stall. If the child refuses what is offered there may be no money in the budget for an alternative (Thurlbeck 2000: 809).

> While poor families are understandably concerned with ensuring that children's stomachs feel full and that they have sufficient calories for energy, repeated studies have shown that coronary heart disease, certain cancers and obesity are linked to nutritionally poor diets in childhood. For children like Jason, adult ill health may well be the legacy from his poor childhood diet. Lack of money for iron rich food such as red meat and green leafy vegetables have also led to outcomes such as iron deficiency anaemia, leading to reduced immunity and greater susceptibility to infection (BMA 1999). Long-term iron deficiency anaemia in children under 5 years has also been linked with a permanent effect on growth rate and cognitive and psychomotor development (Marx 1997).

- more likely to have a childhood accident

Child accidents are the major cause of death for children aged over 1 year in the UK and children from the lowest socio-economic groups are four times more likely to die from an accident and nine times more likely to die from a house fire than a child from a more affluent home (OPCS 1994; Roberts 2000). Children in poorer neighbourhoods are also likely to have less safe places to play and often face increased danger from traffic. The reasons for such a wide differential in morbidity from accidents between the socio-economic groups has been the cause of much speculation. It is most likely that a wide combination of contributory factors interplay in these outcomes. For example, a smoke alarm may seem an unnecessary expense when struggling financially to provide food for the family and perhaps factors, such as depression or lack of awareness of child development, may mean that risks to children are evaluated differently from one family to another.

- less likely to be breast-fed for any length of time

Despite the benefits of being breast-fed being clearly shown by numerous research studies, there is a dramatic contrast in the incidence of breast-feeding, with women in higher socio-economic groups being twice as likely to breast-feed as women in lower social groups (BMA 1999). Research indicates that the physical cognitive and emotional benefits of breast-feeding are many, including less allergies, less infections, less diabetes and promotion of brain and intestinal development (Jenner 1988; James *et al.* 1997).

- more likely to have parents that smoke

Women from social class 5 are four times more likely to smoke in pregnancy than women in social class 1 (Foster *et al.* 1997), resulting in lower birth weight, and an increased risk of sudden infant death syndrome (Leather 1996). In addition, other research has linked parental smoking, in low-income families, to less balanced diets. In families where both parents smoked, 26 per cent reported that they were unable to afford essential dietary items such as vegetables and fruit compared to 9 per cent in low income families where the parents did not smoke (Marsh and McKay 1994). In addition, the prevalence of asthma and chest infections is higher where children passively inhale cigarette smoke (Upton *et al.* 1998). In the case study, Jason's health visitor was clearly concerned about his repeated chest infections and the possible links with passive smoking.

- more likely to have a parent suffering from depression

Although at least 10 per cent of all mothers suffer post-natal depression (Cooper 1991, cited in Roberts 2000), studies indicate that the long-term effects of maternal depression on the cognitive and emotional development of children is more marked where there is socio-economic disadvantage (Murray and Cooper 1997; Petterson and Burke Albers 2001). Some children, like Jason, may find themselves living in a family where a combination of problems such as lack of money, domestic violence and maternal depression constantly interact to negatively influence health.

- less likely to do well at school

Children from disadvantaged backgrounds tend to have lower educational attainments and recent research studies (Duncan *et al.* 1994) have shown clear deleterious links between poverty and children's cognitive abilities, from as early as two years of age (Smith *et al.* 1997). Acheson (1998: 40–1) recommends that more high quality pre-school education should be developed:

> so that it meets, in particular, the needs of disadvantaged families. We also recommend that the benefits of pre-school education to disadvantaged families are evaluated and, if necessary, additional resources are made available to support further development.

The effects of domestic violence on children's health

Domestic violence is prevalent in all socio-economic groups. Studies have indicated that in homes where there is violence towards women, there is also violence towards one or more children in 40–60 per cent of cases (Hughes *et al.* 1989). Between 75 per cent and 90 per cent of violent incidents in the home are thought to be witnessed by children, in itself constituting emotional abuse. Pre-school children living in violent situations may present with behavioural problems or physical responses such as headaches, stomach aches or diarrhoea as well as erratic nursery attendance and poor concentration (Hilberman and Munson 1977). Abrahams (1994) also found a range of emotional health problems, from being frightened and withdrawn to being angry and aggressive. However, the results of trying to leave a violent home often leads to health consequences for children. Living in a refuge or bed and breakfast may well expose children to a change in economic resources, they may have to leave their friends and neighbourhood and some children, especially from ethnic minority groups, may face bullying (Mullender and Morley 1994).

How can these health inequalities be addressed?

The government commissioned an independent inquiry into inequalities in health and the committee chaired by Sir Donald Acheson produced their report in 1998, highlighting three key areas for health improvement:

1. All policies likely to have an impact on health should be evaluated with regards to their impact on health inequalities.
2. A high priority should be given to the health of families with children.
3. Further steps should be taken to improve the living standards of poor families.

The government has pledged to tackle health inequalities and to end child poverty within a generation and raise the threshold for defining poverty from 50 per cent to 60 per cent of median income (DSS 1999b: Howarth *et al.* 1999). The government's policy agenda includes a whole range of initiatives to improve the health of children. The plan is to ensure that a combination of national policy and local action encourages new and innovative partnerships to tackle inequalities.

Following the tragic death of Victoria Climbie, an eight-year-old girl, who was tortured and killed by her aunt and partner, Lord Laming chaired a public inquiry into how Victoria could have received so little protection in England in the twenty-first century. Lord Laming's inquiry heard that Victoria was seen by numerous professionals involved in child health and welfare, but none of them were able to spot the abuse that Victoria was suffering. Lord Laming's (DH2003) report made 106 recommendations for change to children's services. In particular, it was noted that no-one listened to Victoria and professionals did not communicate or work effectively together. Following the Laming Report, a Minister for Children, Margaret Hodge, was appointed and she has a key role in ensuring that professionals work more closely together. The government published the green paper 'Every Child Matters' (DfES 2003) which highlights the government proposals to set up Children's Trusts by 2006 so that professionals can work in multi-disciplinary teams. The spirit of this paper is positive, and is shown in the fact that a children's version has also been published, but the real challenge lies in how effectively this change to working practices can be achieved.

The policy agenda includes:

* reducing child poverty by reforming benefits and tax systems;
* raising awareness of healthy behaviour through the Healthy Schools Programme;
* setting up the National Family and Parenting Institute to value and support family well-being;
* introducing a National Service Framework (NSF) for children's health to ensure consistency of health services for children in all areas and that children and families are consulted about services;
* strengthening the support available to families in disadvantaged areas through Sure Start for families with children under four years of age;
* the Sure Start approach is the foundation for the development of new Children's Centres which will provide a single place where five key services – early education, childcare, health, family support and help into employment, will be offered. The first 32 children's centres were announced in 2003 and the government plans to extend the network across the country.
* setting up the Children's Fund to allow local projects to provide preventative services for 5–13-year-olds and their families;
* improving the health of vulnerable children through the Quality Protects Scheme;
* improving access to healthy food through school breakfast clubs in disadvantaged areas and the National School Fruit Scheme (see example below).

Examples of three interventions to improve children's health

The national school fruit scheme: a national government scheme

During 2001 the Department of Health piloted a National School Fruit Scheme in a cross-section of 500 primary, infant, special and nursery schools. The scheme aims to ensure that every child between four and six years of age is offered a piece of fresh fruit every day. The scheme has been evaluated positively so far, recording comments from teachers like the following:

> It has challenged our misconceptions that children won't eat fruit.

> An excellent filler between breakfast and lunch, especially as certain children have little or no breakfast.

Following early evaluations the government plans to ensure that by 2004 every child will be entitled to a piece of fruit every day at infants' school.

Bright beginnings: a voluntary sector project

The Children and Young People's Participation Project Warrington aims to promote healthy eating and child safety. This Children's Society group meets once a week and is open to anyone in the area who cares for a child of under five years. The group has a rolling programme of activities and carers decide which session they would like. Sessions include:

- Healthy eating
- Eating ideas for children
- Cookery on a budget
- Fun with food

This project is a partner to Warrington child accident group, who recently carried out a campaign called 'Careful, that's Hot' in response to statistics from Warrington Accident and Emergency Department in 2000, showing the extremely high number of injuries to children due to hot drinks and hot fat. The project supports this safety campaign by offering a 'SAFE (Safe Affordable Family Equipment) Buy' outlet, selling safety equipment and offering advice on safety to families. This scheme aims to offer families the knowledge and skills to make their own informed decisions about child safety.

Development of home zones: a local authority safety intervention

Some local authorities are launching 'Home Zone' schemes aimed at ensuring that the local neighbourhood is for people rather than transport. The Northmoor inner city estate in Manchester based their home zone on a consultation with local people. The area is now planted out with trees, there are safe play areas and an improved road layout with traffic calming measures.

A partnership approach

The schemes described above are innovative attempts to try to improve the health and safety of children, but they can only have a real impact on health if they are part of an integrated range of measures. Each initiative needs to add another part to the puzzle of meeting health needs in an holistic way. So, to use the example of developing home zones, this not only provides for safe play in a pleasant environment, it also involves consulting with children, young people and adults to find out what they think will work. By actually participating, people can 'own' the changes and develop personally through meaningful contributions. By actively contributing children and adults feel valued and competent, whereas those living in deprived situations often feel powerless and unable to influence. Sure Start projects are attempting to redress this power imbalance by actively listening and consulting with the community so that services are flexible to fit what parents and children want and need. This chapter now considers Sure Start, in more detail, as a framework for partnership working, with examples of interventions that are being implemented to improve children's emotional and physical health.

The aim of Sure Start

To work with parents-to-be, parents and children to promote the physical, intellectual and social development of babies and young children – particularly those who are disadvantaged – so that they can flourish at home and when they get to school, and thereby break the cycle of disadvantage for the current generation of young children.

(Sure Start 2001: 4)

Sure Start is a radical and innovative strategy aiming to improve the health and well-being of families with children under four years old. Sure Start initiatives are being set up across England and are based on evidence that effective interventions and support can help to prevent family breakdown and promote healthy emotional development and children's readiness to learn.

How can Sure Start improve children's health?

Sure Start staff, from education, health and voluntary sectors are serving communities and helping to organise services in partnership with families. Services aim to reflect local needs and find innovative ways of ensuring that children and families have improved support, easier access to health and education services and involvement in their child's development and early learning. The government aims to fund 500 Sure Start programmes across England by 2004, promoting health and limiting the adverse effects of poverty on children's health. Every family with a new baby in a Sure Start area is offered a home visit to explain what the scheme can offer and many families will be involved before the birth. For example, some Sure Start projects are working with families to prepare them for the emotional changes of the transition to parenthood. Traditionally men and women have learnt about the physical aspects of birth at ante-natal classes (Combes and Schonveld 1992; Underdown 1998a) and are often unprepared for the emotional challenges when a new baby is born (Parr 1996; Underdown 1998b). Parr has shown that preparation that supports communication and relationships in the family when a baby is born reduces stress and anxiety and promotes positive family relationships. The charity set up by Parr, PIPPIN (Parents in Partnership–Parent Infant Network) pioneered classes offering support in the emotional transition to parenthood and some Sure Start areas are working in partnership with PIPPIN. Other work to promote sensitive care and secure emotional attachments includes groups where parents can learn infant massage. The importance of promoting early relationships between parents and infants was highlighted by the Carnegie task force (cited in BMA 1999: 34–5) who identified three factors that could protect against health inequalities within the early years:

- temperament and peri-natal factors (such as full-term birth and normal birth-weight): having characteristics which attract and encourage care giving;
- dependable care givers: growing up in a family with one or two dependable adults who are positive and encouraging;
- community support: living in a loving, supportive and safe community can limit the risk to health.

Why is early support for emotional development important?

There is increasing concern about the high levels of distress and mental health problems experienced by children and young people (*Mental Health Foundation* 1999). The first months of life are a critical period where children are making emotional attachments and forming the crucial first relationships, which lay the foundations for their future mental health. Children who do not form secure attachments (Bowlby 1965) are at far higher risk of developing behavioural problems and emotional difficulties. Early interventions, specifically set up to nurture these first attachments, may well prevent damaging relationship patterns being set up. When babies are small and dependent they rely totally on their care giver to interpret their needs. Thus, the baby will cry and the emotionally available care giver will process what this means and then respond to the baby. For example, a mother who is attuned (Stern 1998) to her baby may come into the baby's view as he lays in his cot saying, in 'sing-song' infant-directed speech: 'Oh dear, dear dear. You are a sad little boy. Did you wake up suddenly and think your tummy was empty? Come and have a big cuddle while I get your milk.' By saying this, the mother is naming her perceptions of the child's emotions and she is attempting to 'contain' the sadness for him. As scenes like this happen daily, the baby gradually forms a picture of a care giver who can be relied on to contain difficult feelings. As children grow they develop an ability to contain their own feelings because their care givers have provided a secure base. Containing a baby's feelings like this is a demanding task for any parent or care giver and relies, to an extent, on the carers having had their own needs met as infants. As Woodhead argues (2001: 3):

> but this is hard, for if a mother has a deep down feeling that no-one was ever able to be thoughtful about her and responsive to her own infant needs. When we add poor economic, material and social circumstances the picture is bleak indeed.

The concept of 'holding' literally means that the parent holds the baby in mind, thinking about how he or she might feel and what his or her needs are. One way of encouraging parents to 'hold' their child in mind is by celebrating together the way the child is learning and developing and noticing the ways that young children communicate through their play, actions and reactions. The Sure Start initiative aims to value and empower parents so that they can begin to achieve their potential and help their children to do the same. Parents who have never been listened to themselves may well find it difficult to 'tune in' to their children but schemes like the 'Growing Together' group (Woodhead 2001), at the Pen Green Centre, aim to support emotional relationships and provide a secure environment for creative learning.

The Pen Green 'Growing Together' Group

The Pen Green 'Growing Together' group is part of the Sure Start provision, in Corby, aiming to support children under three years and their families. The group meets for one and a half hours and typically has an attendance of about 15 mothers/fathers and their babies. There is normally a staff of four who meet beforehand to prepare and think about the provision and practice, it is important that there is a consistency of staff so that relationships can be built and the 'thinking' in the group can be built up over time. Attention is paid to important details, such as ensuring that the group starts and finishes on time and is not cancelled at short notice. Parents are welcomed with a warm drink (safety measures carefully adhered to) and the aim is to nurture parents as well as children. The play provision is carefully set out and parents are encouraged to watch and take pleasure in how their own child learns and plays with others. Children often learn through 'schemas' which are repeated patterns of play. Parents can become expert in identifying the way their children learn and this makes them acutely aware of their needs. Staff use a digital video camera to record the sequences of play, and still images can be printed for parents to take home. The group aims to model the type of play activities which can be used at home and parents will often develop the expertise to extend their child's play at home, knowing that one of the workers and perhaps other parents will be happy to listen and discuss the development. Staff are available to talk confidentially with parents, who sometimes may have strong feelings evoked about their own childhood and, perhaps, not having had their own needs met. This is not a counselling group, but for many parents having someone who values and listens is enough to help them 'work through emotional baggage'. For those who need more help staff can 'signpost' to suitable support. Just as the 'nurture' at the beginning of the group is important, so is separation at the end. Fifteen minutes before the end staff give out bubble blowing equipment, so that the group ends gently with children recognising that the bubbles mean that it is time to clear away and say goodbye.

This group specifically aims 'to support and facilitate the development of emotional attachments and emotionally expressed companionship between care givers and their babies' (Woodhead 2001: 1). The practice is well grounded in theory, particularly attachment theory (Bowlby 1988) and the concepts of containment (Bion 1962) and holding (Winnicott 1960).

What does this mean for early years practitioners?

The national agenda is clearly focused on reducing health inequalities for children and this reflects the need for a change in traditional working practices. Children's services, health, education, social services and the voluntary sector have frequently worked in isolation, despite the fact that partnership working can offer so much to children and families. Partnership with parents requires professionals to share their knowledge and their power and this requires confidence to discover new ways of working.

As one young father explained after his son had fallen down and pushed his teeth into his lip:

> It was bleeding all over the place and he was screaming his head off. I didn't know what to do, then I suddenly thought of his trajectory schema. So I got a cup of water and told him to swill it round his mouth and then spit it as far as he could into the sink. In a minute he was laughing again.

A child who has a trajectory schema (Bruce and Meggitt 1996) is fascinated with things that move or fly through the air such as balls, rockets or aeroplanes. Most people would not know what a trajectory schema is, but that knowledge, gained from a child development group, enabled the father to effectively problem solve. The nursery worker who had shared this knowledge about schemas with the father had done an excellent job in promoting positive mental health.

Early years practitioners have an exciting but challenging opportunity to be involved in interventions which can really improve the long-term health for children. To meet these challenges early years practitioners need the following:

- the confidence to ensure that children and parents are central in informing and participating in initiatives;
- the skills to effectively consult and involve parents and children as equal partners;
- to work effectively with multi-agency staff from the statutory and voluntary sectors, sharing expertise and adopting new ways of working in partnership with families;
- to be responsive to differing community needs, for example, communities may have high unemployment, few people with English as their first language or a

transient family population;
- to consider equality of opportunity issues, for example, where Sure Start is unavailable;
- to disseminate good practice, learned from local programmes, to everyone involved in providing services for young children.

Tragedies like the death of Victoria Climbie must never be allowed to happen again. Services must work effectively together to ensure that children are protected. Sure Start and the new children centres should lead the way in encouraging better communication and partnership working as a basic foundation for building preventative services to improve the health of all young children.

Conclusion

This chapter highlights a number of factors that contribute to health inequalities in early childhood and argues that resolving difficulties in isolation will never be effective. Sure Start is a positive example of an initiative which offers a framework and resources for a range of interventions and plays a major part in the government's plan to reduce health inequalities in the early years. Sure Start aims to prevent difficulties by focusing on pioneering new ways of working in partnership with families with children under four, in some of the most deprived areas of the UK. The 'Growing Together' group is one example of how early relationships can be supported, so that parents can form those crucial attachments and celebrate their own child's development. It is through initiatives like 'Growing Together' or infant massage groups that social support networks can be built and other initiatives, like the projects to support healthy eating and safety, can develop. It is, however, disappointing that Sure Start schemes will still only reach a fraction of the total number of children in need and, indeed, it could widen the gap between one community, which has well-resourced Sure Start facilities, and a neighbouring one, which does not. However, the intention is to develop innovative, evidence-based services in the Sure Start areas and then disseminate this learning to improve services, as appropriate, in other areas.

It is an exciting time for early years practitioners to work together and be creative in facilitating the design of supportive services. It is also a challenge for experts to listen and respond to the views of children and parents. It takes confidence to genuinely share expertise and become equal partners. Children's health is too important to be left to chance and the challenge for early years professionals is to use the rapidly evolving evidence base about what is effective in the early years, and to implement services according to local need. The long-term health benefits of effective early preventative services are likely to far outweigh the short-term costs.

CHAPTER 12

Work, play and learning in the lives of young children

Martin Woodhead

The title of this chapter may seem puzzling at first. If it had been called 'play and learning in the lives of young children', the reader might anticipate familiar themes about the importance of play, and perhaps some discussion about when children should begin more formal learning. In this chapter I make a case for including work – alongside play and learning – in studies of childhood, including early childhood.

'Play is the child's work', so early childhood practitioners sometimes claim (following Susan Isaacs 1929). Their concerns are often about the kinds of learning and teaching that are appropriate for young children. For example, in Britain there's been an ongoing debate about when children should start school (Woodhead 1989), as well as about what curriculum is appropriate, especially for four-year-olds (Miller *et al.* 2002). Should young children be getting started on formal teaching of National Curriculum subjects, especially literacy and numeracy? Or is a play-based curriculum more developmentally appropriate for four-year-olds? Chapters 2 and 3 have debated some of these issues, which are far from new.

History of debates about work, play and learning

To understand the origin of contemporary debates in early years education, we need to go back more than one hundred years, to the establishment of mass schooling. The age of five-years-old was first defined as the starting age for compulsory school by the 1870 and 1880 Education Acts. It was an early start by comparison with other European countries. The decision to send children to school from five was not based solely on considerations about children's learning. The government of the day also had to satisfy those who were worried about losing children from the work force, especially from the agricultural sector. A major reason for setting an early start for compulsory schooling was in order to provide the mass of poor children with a few years intensive schooling before they reached the age when they could play a useful role in the economy, and help support their families. An extract from

Parliamentary debates at the time illustrates the strength of feeling. Here is how one Member of Parliament made his case:

> Send the children to school at five by all means . . . but do not prevent them by force, after they were 10 years old, from earning all they could towards the support of themselves and their little brothers and sisters. (cited in Woodhead 1989: 6)

Starting early in order to finish early was the order of the day! But debates at that time were not only about when children should start school. There were also questions about what young children should be taught and how they should learn. This especially became an issue following the 1870 Act, because of the trend for children even younger than five to join their older brothers and sisters on the benches and galleries of the crowded elementary school classrooms. By 1890, half a million under fives were attending school, very often in conditions that were far from ideal. One commentator, writing in 1891, had a clear vision about what school life should be about in the so-called 'babies class':

> The school life of these little children is organised play. By play they learn the first rudiments of letters. Through play they first discover their own latent powers, and find out how much they can do by imitating what they see others do. To sit with folded arms is an interval of rest in the play-learning of the day. (from The Graphic, *Illustrated London News* 1891)

Other observers were less confident that the schools of the day were able to adapt to the needs of young children. A Ministry of Education Inspector, Katherine Bathurst, describes her impressions of life for the 'babies' in the elementary schools she visited in Manchester, England in 1905.

> He often cannot reach the floor with his feet, and in many cases he has no back to lean against. He is told to fold his arms and sit quiet. He is surrounded by a large number of other babies all under similar alarming and incomprehensible conditions, and the effort to fold his arms is by no means conducive to comfort or well being. (cited in Van der Eyken 1973: 120, 122)

Contemporary classrooms may be more suited for young children in lots of ways, but underlying concerns about young children being expected to make an early start on 'school work' echo those debates of a hundred years ago (Elkind 1985; Woodhead 1989). Towards the end of the chapter I will return to the issue whether some kinds of school learning should rightly be seen as a form of child work.

But I also want to ask about young children 'working' in a more conventional sense, in economic activity. As noted above, decisions made in 1870 about the age when children should start school were closely tied to beliefs about when they should begin productive life, as young workers. By that time, the principle of universal schooling had been agreed. But, if we step back another century, young children were being seen as already ready for work. The social historian Hugh Cunningham notes:

> Until the late eighteenth century it had been axiomatic in all societies that most children should in some way contribute to economic production from an early age . . . Daniel Defoe, in the 1720s commended those textile producing areas of England where 'the very children after 4 or 5 years of age could every one earn their own bread'. John Locke, who . . . enjoyed a reputation for enlightened views towards child rearing and education thought that children whose parents were unable to support them should be sent to a working school at the age of 3, to be inured to habits of hard labor. (1996: 31–2)

Defoe and Locke were talking in the eighteenth century about children of the same age and developmental stage as the children who sat with their brothers and sisters on the benches and galleries of the crowded nineteenth-century classrooms. In the same way, the children engaged in play-based learning in traditional British nursery schools and playgroups for most of the past 50 years are the same age and stage as the children now being introduced to structured activities based on the Foundation Stage curriculum guidance in England (QCA 2000).

One of the lessons from these historical accounts is about the many competing ways early childhood has been and is currently constructed in discourses and practices, even within one society. While children of three and four years old share features of physical growth and maturity, adult expectations for their activities, relationships and learning vary enormously, which shapes the ways they are treated, in terms of diverse beliefs about what is a quality childhood (Woodhead 1996).

The place of work in young children's lives

Few young children work in contemporary Britain, in the literal sense of paid employment, with the possible exception of the babies and toddlers recruited to appear on TV, in films and especially in advertising – everything from nappies to mineral water! But it is meaningful to talk about work in the sense of young children's contributions to the household and community – however modest, immature and playful. And work isn't just playful for most of the world's children, especially during the middle and later years of childhood. In this section, I will look briefly at child work in general, before turning specifically to the place of work in young children's lives.

The world's children do many different kinds of work, including household chores, agricultural work, fishing, market portering, street trading, shoe-shining, mining, craft workshops and engineering, rubbish picking, domestic work, and prostitution (Woodhead 1999a). Most public attention is rightly focused on the most exploitative and hazardous kinds of child labour, mostly in the poorest countries of the world. One unfortunate consequence can be that the more moderate kinds of work done by the vast majority of children is overlooked. It is also widely assumed that school is now a universal experience of childhood. But it is estimated that about one fifth of the world's children never go to school (Watkins 2000).

Finally, school is not an alternative to work for most of the world's children, many of whom combine work with school. They have to work to support their families, and sometimes to help pay some of the costs of going to school (Boyden *et al.* 1998).

To get an impression of the significance of children's economic contribution Hoffman *et al.* (1987) asked parents in eight countries about the value they placed on their children: 75 per cent of Thai parents, 71 per cent of parents in the Philippines, 54 per cent in Turkey referred to children's value as contributors to the family income, compared with only 6 per cent of US parents. Parents in the USA were much more likely to refer to the emotional significance of having children, the stimulation and fun involved (see also Zelizer 1985).

In a similar study carried out in Cameroon, West Africa, parents valued children for their ability to do domestic chores (56 per cent), and run errands (30 per cent) (Nsamenang and Lamb 1993). In these poor, mainly rural economies, young children are not just playful dependants, who are growing and learning, towards some future goal of mature competence when they are ready to enter the workforce. They are an essential, trainable, economic resource, contributing now, and even more so as they get older.

Cross-cultural studies of young children's work

These statistics are about children in general. What about the youngest children – where do they fit in? Samantha Punch carried out a detailed study of children's work in Churquiales, a small rural community in southern Bolivia. She observed children in 18 households, interviewing parents and grandparents as well as children. She also accompanied children during the activities of their day and used photographs, drawings and mapping techniques. She found even the youngest children were expected to contribute to household chores, animal care and agriculture. By three or four years old, children were already fetching water, collecting firewood, going on errands, feeding ducks and chickens, scaring birds from crops, picking peas and beans, peeling maize stalks and harvesting peaches. As children got older they progressed onto more complex, physically demanding and responsible tasks. Through observation and questioning, Punch drew up a list of what might be called 'key stages in the curriculum' for work among these rural children. A summary of some of tasks expected of each age group is given in Table 12.1.

Punch also notes for this rural Bolivian society that initially there was not a clear division of labour by gender, but that gradually the expectations on boys and girls diverge. Punch concludes:

Even from an early age children carry out some tasks independently and they should not be seen purely as helpers but active contributors in their own right. Their unpaid work not only benefits the household . . . but also increases their sense of autonomy, enabling them to gain skills and competencies useful for their individual independence. (2001: 818)

Table 12.1 Children's work in a rural community in Bolivia

Domestic work	Agricultural tasks	Animal care
3–5 years: Fetching water, collecting firewood, running errands	4–6 years: Picking vegetables, harvesting peaches, peeling maize stalks	3–6 years: Feeding ducks and chickens, scaring birds from crops
6–7 years: Bed-making, cleaning and sweeping, peeling potatoes, washing dishes	7–9 years: Sowing seeds, watering crops, weeding, harvesting maize	7–9 years: Looking after pigs, milking and feeding goats, and cows, plucking a chicken
8–9 years: Lighting fire and simple food preparation; looking after younger siblings	10–12 years: Preparing ground for planting, hoeing, fertilising, harvesting potatoes	10–13 years: Harnessing oxen for ploughing, killing a chicken for eating, skinning a pig
10/11+ years: Washing clothes, making main meals, including bread, shopping for household	13–14 years: Ploughing, clearing forest land, Storing maize	14+years: Loading up a donkey securely, taking cattle to forest pastures, killing a goat or pig

Source: Adapted from Punch (2001: 811–12)

In other societies, expectations of work may be very different of course. For example, girls and boys' work may be segregated much earlier. Occupational roles may be linked to children's social class/caste as well as their age and gender (Blanchett 1996). In some traditional communities, children may be apprenticed to learn a particular trade from an early age, which becomes the main focus for their daily lives and their learning. For example, in certain communities in Bangladesh, young boys are regularly engaged in learning hand embroidering in small workshops (Woodhead 1999a).

These specific examples of young children working are borne out by a larger-scale cross-cultural study in Mexico, the Philippines, Kenya, Japan and the USA (Whiting and Whiting 1975). In several of these communities it is considered normal, appropriate and desirable for children to contribute to chores from the age of 3 or 4, with much lower expectations of children in countries like Japan and the USA. But this research also cautions against simplistic dichotomies between the conditions of children in so-called modern and so-called traditional societies. Each socio-economic context is associated with a particular pattern of parental expectations, and there may be substantial diversity in beliefs within any one context.

Among hunter-gather society studied by Draper (1976), the !Kung San, children aged 4–9 devoted only 3 per cent of their time to work tasks.

From a Western perspective, child work is viewed as a potential threat to children's welfare and development. The expression 'child labour' is frequently used, which has connotations of exploitation and harm. From his research among the Abaluyia of Kenya, Weisner (1989) notes that parents may hold a quite contrary view. Children's work is seen as valuable, not just in preparing them for their adult roles, but serving an essential function as a form of emotional and social support, integrating children into a family and community network that places high value on interdependence and interconnectedness. The absence of a productive economic function for young family members in industrialised societies has its own repercussions:

> Western children do not begin to learn the occupational competencies they will need as adults until late adolescence or early adulthood, and often are not prepared for adult responsibilities until about the same time. This continuity may contribute to feelings of alienation and aimlessness experienced by many adolescents and described by many social scientists. (Tietjen 1989: 406)

Are early childhoods in Europe and North America work-free?

Clearly, the role of children in economically advanced societies, such as in Europe and North America, is very different from Bolivia, Kenya or the Philippines. But are early childhoods in the West quite so 'work-free' as these contrasts suggest? Dominant discourses of early childhood development emphasise the early years as a period of dependency and playful innocence (Woodhead 1999b). Research that has looked more closely at children's social lives tells a slightly different story. For example, Judy Dunn has drawn attention to very young children's interest and engagement in family activities, events and dramas. Children as young as two years old were observed to show sensitivity to the needs of others, trying to help a sibling or parent in distress (Dunn 1988). Not long after I graduated from university, I stayed with a family with a three-year-old. I remember being fascinated by the way the child watched her mother doing chores in the kitchen and followed her father around the garden, carrying a miniature watering can. Some years later, our first child, then aged about four, was determined to help me spread concrete for a new garden path, with the inevitable messy (and quick-setting) outcome! I now recognise his assertive demands 'Me do it' were not just about wanting to play. He wanted to contribute to the project and to learn the skills needed to do it.

A study by Harriet Rheingold carried out in the USA, confirms very young children's enthusiasm to contribute to domestic tasks, even in societies with a culture of childhood which emphasises children's playfulness. She observed mothers carrying out domestic chores with their toddlers present, e.g. laying the table, sweeping the floor, tidying newspapers:

All the children, even those as young as 18 months of age, promptly and for the most part without direction participated in some everyday housekeeping tasks performed by adults . . . In declaring their intentions to carry out contributing behaviors and in promptly leaving a task on its completion, as well as in verbalizing the accomplishment of the goal – behaviors that increased with age – they showed an awareness of themselves as working jointly with adults to a recognised end. (Rheingold 1982: 122–3)

These examples illustrate young children's intrinsic interest in contributing to, participating in and learning from shared activities with parents and others. In modern societies, young children's contributions to household work are restricted by any number of factors: working patterns in which parents are employed outside the home and children spend time in nursery; convenience food lifestyle and labour-saving devices, the dominance of TV and other modern media. Parents' expectations of young children are also very different, although there are significant variations among social, cultural and ethnic groups. In any case, as high technology is encouraging more home-working among adults, so children's ability to take an interest in work may increase. Beach (1988) found that as soon as children in a US community were able to talk, they showed abilities to understand the rudiments of their parents' work, describing procedures and naming tools, etc. In short, most young children's activities are interpreted within the dominant discourse of 'play' and 'learning'. From the children's point of view they are experienced as attempts to contribute, as small examples of 'work'.

Developmental niches for work, play and learning

The concept of 'developmental niche' provides a useful framework for exploring how universal features of children's development are culturally patterned in diverse ways. Originally proposed by Super and Harkness (1986) in order to make sense of cross-cultural comparisons between communities in Kenya and the USA, the 'developmental niche' draws attention to three components of children's environment:

1. *The physical and social settings they inhabit.* This includes who they live with (in terms of family patterns, peer groups, etc.); the space, organisation and resources in their domestic, play, school and work environments; and the basic schedules of eating, sleeping, studying, working, etc.
2. *The culturally regulated customs and child-rearing practices.* This includes the way parents and others arrange child care and education, the way they relate to the child, instruct them, train them or play with them, their approach to discipline and punishment, etc.
3. *The beliefs or 'ethnotheories' of parents, or others.* This includes goals and priorities for children's development and socialisation, and beliefs or discourses about how they can best be achieved, and indeed how far they are able to influence their children's future.

One of the strengths of this framework is that it recognises the power of cultural beliefs, and discourses in shaping the ways young children's development is understood, which in turn informs the ways they are treated, the skills they learn and their emerging identity. Take motor development, for example. At first sight this might seem a universal developmental process, with young children increasing their skill in eye–hand co-ordination, physical competence, strength and mobility. Motor development also has social purposes. Acts of giving and receiving have been observed in very young infants:

> No parent and no observer can fail to be aware of how often very young children show, offer, and give objects to others. Often such gestures appear to be social overtures . . . As soon as children can walk they will stagger over to someone, especially if that person is unfamiliar, and offer an object. (Dunn 1988: 99)

The way these emergent skills become integrated in children's development depends on the way the young child's initiatives are patterned within the developmental niche – followed-up, given content, meaning and purpose. In Western contexts, motor co-ordination is practised through grasping rattles, playing with 'activity centres', assembling Lego blocks, laying out Brio trains or dressing Barbie dolls. Mobility is marked by learning to sit on trikes, and push trucks, although free exploration is constrained by the dangers of the street and traffic, and increasingly institutionalised within a specialised nursery or kindergarten environment (Singer 1992). In non-industrial niches these skills are practised through play with natural objects, everyday household items or tools. Among the poorest communities in South Asia some families survive by breaking bricks for use as aggregate in house and road building. A brick-chipper's child may start to practise hitting bricks with a small hammer, at an age when other children are hitting wooden or plastic pegs into a block of holes, with equal enthusiasm. The following comment is from a girl in Bangladesh thinking back to her earliest experiences, sitting alongside her mother surrounded by the piles of bricks: 'When I was a child, I used to cry for a hammer. So my mother bought me a hammer and I started breaking bricks' (Woodhead 1998: 35). In this case, it is hard to separate the study of children's work, play and learning from moral questions about children's rights to be protected from harm. Brick breaking is a hazardous job for any child (or indeed adult) to be doing, monotonous, dusty and without protective clothing.

Another example of cultural patterning within the developmental niche is less controversial – the example mentioned above of the three-year-old girl carrying a miniature watering can around the garden. In suburban England (where I made that observation) the child's enthusiasm for watering the plants is likely to be seen as a playful activity, an activity of shared fun with her father. Not too much attention would have been paid to whether the water landed on a clump of dandelions or on the prize dahlias. Transpose the activity to the rural Bolivian community studied by Samantha Punch. According to her research, a young child's involvement in watering the crops would also be treated with a degree of indulgence, with older siblings and parents praising the child's efforts. The difference here is that the child's initial attempts at plant watering are the beginnings of acquiring the skills and responsibility to contribute to productive agriculture, which is crucial to the economic life of the community. Finally, transpose the same activity to a nursery class, where the child pouring water will probably be understood as part of their increased co-ordination skills as well as their understanding about the properties of liquids.

Participation in culturally valued activities

The examples above have in common that they involve young children learning valued skills from sharing in an activity. Barbara Rogoff has made a close study of the way children's growing competencies are incorporated into the cultural life of a child's environment through a process of 'guided participation' (Rogoff 1990). She identifies three features of guided participation:

1. *Collaborative structuring of the situation.* Parents and other care-givers are active in structuring children's environment according to their perceived goals for development. There are several levels of structure. At a macro-level is the overall timetable of the child's day (the balance of time for play, tasks, feeding, washing, resting, etc.). At a micro-level is the way specific tasks and activities are adapted to the perceived capacities of the child, broken down into manageable elements and scaffolded through interactions. These enable the child to achieve a goal or complete a task even though they may not be able to do so on their own yet. In the watering can example, macro-structuring would be about how far watering the plants is a structured part of daily routines. Micro-structure would be about the extent to which the adult or other more skilled partner assists the child to fill up the watering can, or helps them to hold it effectively.

2. *Making connections between the known and the new.* When children encounter a new situation, their care-givers help them to make sense of it in terms of past experiences. So the adult might talk with the child about previous times the child has watered plants, perhaps in a friend's garden. Or they might relate the current experience to other activities with water, such as collecting water from a river, or filling washing bowls with water.

3. *Transferring of responsibility.* Children gradually become more competent in each component of a skill, at which point the adult or more skilled partner typically adjusts their role to give the child more responsibility for carrying out the task. So, another day, the child might be asked to water some plants alone, but with the adult observing at a distance, ready to intervene and re-scaffold the activity if necessary.

Comparing early childhoods in Guatemala, India, Turkey and the USA, Rogoff argues that processes of guided participation are universal, but that important variations are related to the goals of development, and the relationship between children and adults. She highlights the contrasting experiences of developing skills and competencies between societies (e.g. in Britain or North America), where young children's lives are largely separated from adults' economic activity, compared with societies (e.g. the Bolivian community described above) where children observe and participate in ongoing adult activities, including work:

> In communities where they are segregated from adult activities, children's learning may be organized by adults' teaching of lessons and provision of motivational management out of the context of adult practice; in communities in which children are integrated in adult settings, learning can occur through active observation and participation by the children with responsive assistance from caregivers. (Rogoff *et al.* 1993)

Lessons for early childhood

Most research and debate about early childhood takes place in economically rich Western societies in Europe, North America and Australasia. A major focus of debate is on children's play and learning, and this is also the subject of most research. Setting these early childhood issues in an historical as well as cross-cultural context draws attention to other claims for early childhood, related to children's current contribution and future economic activity. Through the examples in this chapter, I have drawn attention to ways that universal features of early development are channelled differently according to context, in terms of cultural priorities for children's work, play and learning. Set in a broad global context, early childhoods in economically advanced societies represent a rather specialised developmental niche, within which discourses about children's dependency, play and learning dominate, to the exclusion of any concept of work. I have tried to show that work – in the broad sense of contributing to household, family and community – has been important and continues to be so for many of the world's children.

In arguing for the inclusion of work in debates about early childhood, I am not advocating that children should be expected to work. In extreme cases, child work is undoubtedly harmful to children's well-being, and rightly condemned. But in many societies children's work is valued by parents, and closely linked to children's socialisation into culturally valued skills. For many of the poorest communities, children's work is essential for families to survive. For these reasons, there is a good case for including the study of children's work alongside their play and learning in early childhood studies.

School as work

At the beginning of this chapter, I said I would come back to the question – how far is school learning itself a form of work? Parents in industrialised societies do not place high expectations on children's economic contribution, but they do have high expectations – for children to work hard and achieve high returns in terms of school achievement. The sociologist, Jens Qvortrop has argued that school work is not as separate from economic activity as we like to think:

> Exactly as children were useful with their hands in an economic formation in which manual labour dominated, children remain useful with mental activities . . . Children are active contributors to human capital formation, and it is important to stress that their school work is useful even while it takes place; indeed if children did not do this school work, society would soon cease to function. (Qvortrop 1998)

According to Qvortrop, children are economically productive when they do school work. They are producing themselves as the future educated work force (Qvortrop 2001). Expectations related to school learning have displaced expectations related to work in modern views of child development. Neither work nor school are 'natural' routes through childhood. Both are culturally created environments that are adaptive to particular economic and cultural priorities.

Acknowledgements

Sections of this chapter draw on a study carried out by the author for Radda Barnen, Save the Children Sweden, published in the reports *Children's Perspectives on their Working Lives* (Stockholm: Radda Barnen, 1998), and *Is There a Place for Work in Child Development?* (Stockholm: Radda Barnen, 1999).

References

Abberley, P. (1987) 'The concept of oppression and the development of a social theory of disability', *Disability, Handicap and Society* 2 (1), 5–19.

Abrahams, C. (1994) *The Hidden Victims: Children and Domestic Violence*. London: NCH Action for Children.

Acheson, D. (1998) *Independent Inquiry into Inequalities in Health Report*. London: HMSO.

Adams, E. (2001) *Power Drawing*. Drawing Power The Campaign for Drawing.

Allen and Chisholm, (2001) in Brundrett, M., Duncan, D. and Silcock P. (eds) *The Primary School Curriculum: Developing Effective Teaching*. Norfolk: Peter Francis.

Anning, A. and Edwards, A. (1999) *Promoting Children's Learning from Birth to Five*. Buckingham: Open University Press.

Athey, C. (1990) *Extending Thought in Young Children: A Parent-teacher Partnership*. London: Paul Chapman.

Audit Commission (1996) *Counting to Five: Education of Children Under Five*. London: HMSO.

Baghban, M. (1984) *Our Daughter Learns to Read and Write*. Newark, DE: International Reading Association.

Ball, C. (1994) *Start Right*. London: Royal Society of Arts.

Base, G. (1986) *Animalia*. New York: Harry Abrams.

Beach, B. (1988) 'Children at work: the home workplace', *Early Childhood Research Quarterly* 3, 209–21.

BEAM (1997) *Learning Mathematics in the Nursery: Desirable Approaches*. London: BEAM/Early Childhood Mathematics Group Publication.

Beard, R. (1999) 'Influences on the Literacy Hour', *Reading: A Journal about Literacy and Language in Education* 33 (1), 6–12.

Beetlestone, F. (1998) *Creative Children, Imaginative Teaching*. Buckingham: Open University Press.

Bennett N., Wood, L. and Rogers, S. (1997) *Teaching Through Play*. Buckingham: Open University Press.

Berefelt, G. (1987) 'Sex differences in scribbles of toddlers: graphic activity of 18 month old children', *Scandinavian Journal of Educational Research*, 31, 23–30.

Bion, W. (1962) *Learning from Experience*. London: Heinemann.

Bissex, G.L. (1980) *Gnys at Wrk: A Child Learns to Read and Write.* Cambridge, MA: Harvard University Press.

Blanchett, T. (1996) *Lost Innocence, Stolen Childhoods.* Dhaka: University of Dhaka Press.

Blenkin, G.M. and Kelly, A.V. (1996) 'Education as development', in Blenkin, G.M. and Kelly, A.V. (eds) *Early Childhood Education: A Developmental Curriculum.* 2nd edn, London: Paul Chapman, pp. 1–28.

BMA (British Medical Association) (1999) *Growing up in Britain: Ensuring a Healthy Future for our Children.* London: BMA.

Bourne, J. (2001) 'Doing "what comes naturally": how the discourses and routines of teachers' practice constrain opportunities for bilingual support in UK primary schools', *Language and Education* **15** (4), 250–68.

Bowlby, J. (1965) *Child Care and the Growth of Love.* Middlesex: Open University Books.

Bowlby, J. (1988) *A Secure Base.* London: Routledge.

Boyden, J., Ling, B. and Myers, W. (1998) *What Works for Working Children.* Stockholm: Radda Barnen.

Bright Futures (1999) London: The Mental Health Foundation.

Brown, R. (1973) *A First Language: The Early Stages.* Cambridge, MA: Harvard University Press.

Browne, A. (1996) *Developing Language and Literacy 3–8.* London: Paul Chapman.

Browne, A. (1998) 'Provision for reading for four year old children', *Reading* **32** (1) 9–13.

Bruce, T. (1987) *Early Childhood Education.* London: Hodder and Stoughton.

Bruce, T. (1991) *Time to Play in Early Childhood Education.* Sevenoaks: Hodder and Stoughton.

Bruce, T. (1997) *Early Childhood Education.* London: Hodder and Stoughton.

Bruce, T. and Meggitt, C. (1996) *Child Care and Education.* London: Hodder and Stoughton.

Bruner, J. (1968) 'Two modes of thought', in Mercer, J. (ed.) *Language and Literacy from an Educational Perspective.* Vol. 1: *Language Studies.* Milton Keynes: Open University Press.

Bruner, J. (1970) 'The course of cognitive growth', in Klintz, B.L. and Brunig, J. (eds), *Research in Psychology.* New York: Scott, Foresman and Co., pp. 289–96.

Bruner, J. (1975) *Toward a Theory of Instruction.* Cambridge, MA: Harvard University Press.

Bruner, J.S. (1986) *Actual Minds, Possible Worlds.* Cambridge, MA: Harvard University Press.

Butler, D. (1998) *Babies Need Books: Sharing the Joy of Books with Children from Birth to Six.* Rev. edn. Portsmouth, NH: Heinemann.

Campbell, R. (1996) *Literacy in Nursery Education.* Stoke-on-Trent: Trentham Books.

Campbell, R. (1999*) Literacy from Home to School: Reading with Alice.* Stoke-on-Trent: Trentham Books.

Campbell, R. (2001a) *Read-Alouds with Young Children.* Newark, DE: International Reading Association.

Campbell, R. (2001b) '"That's how I used to write my name when I was little": under fives exploring writing', in Evans, J. (ed.) *The Writing Classroom: Aspects of Writing and the Primary Child 3–11.* London: David Fulton.

Campbell, R. (2001c) '"I can write my name I can": The importance of the writing of own name', *Education 3–13* **29** (1), 9–14.

Campbell, R. (2002) *Reading in the Early Years Handbook.* 2nd edn. Buckingham: Open University Press.

Carpenter, B. (ed.) (1997) *Families in Context: Emerging Trends in Family Support and Early Intervention.* London: David Fulton.

Carr, M. and May, H. (2000) 'Te Whaariki: curriculum voices', in Penn, H. (ed.) *Early Childhood Services: Theory, Policy and Practice.* Buckingham: Open University Press, pp. 53–73.

CCEA (1999) *Key Messages from the Curriculum 21 Conferences and the Curriculum Monitoring Programme 1998.* Belfast: Northern Ireland Council for the Curriculum, Examinations and Assessment.

Chisholm, A.J. (2001) Unpublished paper, presented at the University of Hertfordshire.

Chukovsky, K. (1963) *From Two to Five.* Berkeley, CA: University of California Press.

Clay, M. (1985) *The Early Detection of Reading Difficulties.* 3rd edn. Auckland: Heinemann.

Clement, R. *et al.* (1998) *Coordinating Art across the Primary School.* London: Falmer Press.

Collingwood, R.G. (1994) *The Idea of History.* Revised edn. Oxford: Oxford University Press.

Combes, G. and Schonveld, A. (1992) *Life Will Never Be the Same Again.* London: Health Education Authority.

Cooper, H. (1995) *Teaching History in the Early Years.* London: Routledge.

Cooper, Y. (2001) *Tackling Health Inequalities: Consultation on a Plan for Delivery.* London: HMSO.

Corden, R. (2000) *Literacy and Learning through Talk Strategies for the Primary Classroom.* Buckingham: Open University Press.

Costello, P. (2000) *Thinking Skills and Early Years Education.* London: David Fulton.

Cox, M. (1992) *Children's Drawings.* London: Penguin.

Cox, M. (1997) *Drawings of People by the Under-5s.* London: Falmer Press.

Cummins, J. (1984) *Bilingualism and Special Education: Issues in Assessment and Pedagogy.* Clevedon: Multilingual Matters.

Cunningham, C. and Davis, H. (1985) *Working with Parents: Frameworks for Collaboration.* Milton Keynes: Open University Press.

Cunningham, H. (1996) 'The history of childhood', in Lamb, M., Hwang P. and Sigel, S. (eds) *Images of Childhood.* New Jersey: Lawrence Erlbaum.

David, T. (1990) *Under Five – Under Educated?* Milton Keynes: Open University Press.

David, T. and Nurse, A. (1999) 'Inspection of under fives education and constructions of early childhood', in David, T. (ed.) *Teaching Young Children.* London: Paul Chapman.

David, T., Raban, B., Ure, C., Gouch, K., Jago, M., Barriere, I. and Lambirth, A. (2000) *Making Sense of Early Literacy: A Practitioner's Perspective.* Stoke on Trent: Trentham Books.

Department for Education and Employment (1997a) *Guidance 1998–1999: Early Years Development Plans and Partnerships.* Darlington: Department for Education and Employment.

Department for Education and Employment (1997b) *Excellence for All Children: Meeting Special Educational Needs.* London: The Stationery Office.

Department for Education and Employment (1998a) *The National Literacy Strategy: Framework for Teaching.* London: Department for Education and Employment.

Department for Education and Employment (1998b) *Meeting Special Educational Needs: A Programme of Action.* London: DfEE.

Department for Education and Employment (1999a) *The National Literacy Strategy: Additional Literacy Support.* Modules 1–4. London: Department for Education and Employment.

Department for Education and Employment (1999b) *The National Numeracy Strategy.* London: Department for Education and Employment.

Department for Education and Employment (2000) *Foundation Degrees: Consultation Paper.* London: Department for Education and Employment.

Department for Education and Employment (2001) *Sessional Care: National Standards for Under Eights Day Care and Childminding.* London: Department for Education and Employment.

Department for Education and Employment/Qualifications and Curriculum Authority (1999) *The National Curriculum.* London: Department for Education and Employment/Qualifications and Curriculum Authority.

Department for Education and Skills (2001a) *Statement of Requirement.* London: Department for Education and Skills.

Department for Education and Skills (2001b) *Special Educational Needs Code of Practice.* London: DFES.

Department for Education and Skills (2001c) *The Special Educational Needs and Disability Act.* London: HMSO.

Department for Education and Skills (2003) *Every Child Matters.* London: The Stationery Office.

Department for Health (1991) *The Children Act (1989) Guidance and Regulations. Vol 2. Family Support, Day Care and Educational Provision for Young Children.* London: HMSO.

Department of Education and Science (1967) *Children and their Primary Schools.* (The Plowden Report). London: HMSO.

Department of Education and Science (1978) *The Warnock Report: Special Educational Needs.* London: HMSO.

Department of Education and Science (1981) *The Education Act, 1981.* London: HMSO.

Department of Education and Science (1990) *Starting with Quality.* London: HMSO.

Department of Health (2003) *Keeping Children Safe.* London: The Stationery Office.

Department of Social Security (1999a) *Households Below Average Income: A Statistical Analysis 1979–1995/96.* London: HMSO.

Department of Social Security (1999b) *Opportunity for All: Tackling Poverty and Social Exclusion, The First Annual Report.* London: HMSO.

Dodd, L. (1990) *Slinky Malinki.* Harmondsworth: Puffin Books.

Donaldson, M. (1978) *Children's Minds.* London: Collins.

Draper, P. (1976) 'Social and economic constraints on child life among the !Kung', in Lee, Richard B. and Devore, Irven (eds) *Kalahari Hunter-gatherers: Studies of the !Kung*

San and Their Neighbors. Cambridge, MA: Harvard University Press.

Drury, R., Miller, L. and Campbell, R. (2000) *Looking at Early Years Education and Care.* London: David Fulton.

Duckworth, E. (1987) *The Having of Wonderful Ideas.* New York: Teachers College Press.

Duncan, G., Brooks-Gunn, J. and Klebanov, P. (1994) 'Economic deprivation and early childhood development', *Child Development* **65** (2), 296–318.

Dunn, J. (1988) *The Beginnings of Social Understanding.* Oxford: Blackwell.

Duffy, B. (1998) *Supporting Creativity and Imagination in the Early Years.* Buckingham: Open University Press.

Education Review Office (2000) *Early Literacy and Numeracy: The Use of Assessment to Improve Programmes for Four to Six Year Olds.* http://www.ero.govt.nz/Publications/pubs/2000/earlylit&num.htm

Edwards, B. (1988) *Drawing on the Artist Within: How to Release Your Hidden Creativity.* London: Collins.

Edwards, B. (1992) *Drawing on the Right Side of the Brain: How to Unlock Your Hidden Artistic Talent.* London: HarperCollins.

Edwards, E. and Knight, P. (1996) *Effective Early Years Education.* Buckingham: Open University Press.

EEC (2000) *Early Years: The Report on the Proceedings of the Committee and the Education Sub-Committee relating to the Report.* London: The Stationery Office (online). www.publications.parliament.uk/pa/cm200001/cmselect/cmeduemp/33/3302.htm

Elkind, D. (1985) *The Hurried Child.* Reading, MA: Addison-Wesley.

Ellis, R. (1988) 'The effects of linguistic environment on the second language acquisition of grammatical rules', *Applied Linguistics* **9** (3), 257–73.

Elstgeest, J. (1985) 'The right question at the right time', in Harlen, W. (ed.) *Primary Science: Taking the Plunge.* London: Heinemann, pp. 36–46.

Fawcett, M. and Calder, P. (1998) 'Early childhood studies degrees', in Abbott, L. and Pugh, G. (eds) *Training to Work in the Early Years.* Buckingham: Open University Press.

Foster, K., Lader, D. and Cheesborough, S. (1997) *Infant Feeding.* London: HMSO.

Franke, R.H. and Kaul, J.D. (1978) 'The Hawthorne experiments: first statistical interpretation', *American Sociological Review* **43**, 623–43.

Furneaux, B. (1988) *Special Parents.* Milton Keynes: Open University Press.

Gardner, H. (1980) *Artful Scribbles: The Significance of Children's Drawings.* London: Jill Norman.

Gergen, K. (1985) 'The social constructionist movement in modern psychology', *American Psychologist* **40**, 266–75.

Gifford, S. (1995) 'Number in early childhood', in *Early Childhood Development and Care* **109**: 95–119.

Goodey, C. (1991) *Living in the Real World: Families Speak about Down's Syndrome.* London: The Twenty-One Press.

Goodey, C. (1992) 'Fools and heretics: parents' views of professionals', in Booth, T. *et al. Policies for Diversity in Education,* London: Routledge, pp. 165–76.

Goodnow, J. (1977) *Children's Drawing: The Developing Child.* London: Collins/Open Books.

Gregory, E. (1996) *Making Sense of a New World: Learning to Read in a Second Language.* London: Paul Chapman.

Gregory, S. and Bishop, J. (1989) 'The integration of deaf children into ordinary schools: a research report', *The Journal of the British Association of Teachers of the Deaf* 13, 1, 1–6.

Gregory, S., Bishop, J. and Sheldon, L. (1995) *Deaf Young People and Their Families.* Cambridge: Cambridge University Press.

Hall, N. (1987) *The Emergence of Literacy.* Sevenoaks: Edward Arnold.

Hall, N. and Abbott, L. (ed.) (1991) *Play in the Primary Curriculum.* London: Hodder and Stoughton.

Halliday, M.K.H. (1975) *Learning How to Mean.* London: Arnold.

Hamers, J.-F. and Blanc, M. (1989) *Bilinguality and Bilingualism.* Cambridge: Cambridge University Press.

Harlen, W. (2000) *The Teaching of Science in Primary Schools.* 3rd edn. London: David Fulton.

Harré, R. (1986) *Varieties of Realism.* Oxford: Blackwell.

Harris, M. (1992) *Language Experience and Early Language Development: From Input to Uptake.* Hove: Lawrence Erlbaum Associates.

Harris, R.J. (ed.) (1992) *Cognitive Processing in Bilinguals: Advances in Psychology 83.* Amsterdam: North-Holland.

Hendrick, J. (1997) *First Steps Toward Teaching the Reggio Way.* Englewood Cliffs, NJ: Prentice-Hall.

Hevey, D. and Curtis, A. (1996) 'Training to work in the early years', in Pugh, G. (ed.) *Contemporary Issues in the Early Years.* London: Paul Chapman.

Hexter, G.H. (1972) *The History Primer.* London: Allen Lane.

Hilberman, E. and Munson, K. (1977) 'Sixty battered women', *Victimology: An International Journal* 2 (3–4), 460–70.

Holdaway, D. (1979) *The Foundations of Literacy.* London: Ashton Scholastic.

Hopwood, V. and Gallaway, C. (1999) 'Evaluating the linguistic experience of a deaf child in a mainstream class: a case study', *Deafness and Education International* 3, 3, 172–87.

Hoffman, L.W. (1987) 'The value of children to parents and child rearing patterns', in Kagitcibasi, C. (ed.) *Growth and Progress in Cross-cultural Psychology.* Berwyn: Swets N. America Inc.

Howarth, C., Kenway, P., Palmer, R. and Miorellie, R. (1999) *Monitoring Poverty and Social Exclusion.* York: Joseph Rowntree Foundation.

http://wwwpublications.parliament.uk/pa/cm200001/cmselect/cmeduemp/33/3303.htm

Hughes, H., Parkinson, D. and Vargo, M. (1989) 'Witnessing spouse abuse and experiencing physical abuse: a double whammy?', *Journal of Family Violence* 4, 197–209.

Hughes, M. (1986) *Children and Number.* Oxford: Blackwell.

Hutchins, P. (1972) *Good-Night Owl.* London: The Bodley Head.

Isaacs, N. (1958) 'Early scientific trends in children'. Opening lecture at a course on 'The foundations of scientific attitudes: their development in the primary School', University of Reading, Reading.

Isaacs, S. (1929) *The Nursery Years.* London: Routledge and Kegan Paul.

James, W., Nelson, M. and Ralph, A. (1997) 'Socio-economic determinants of health: the contribution of nutrition to inequalities in health', *British Medical Journal*, 314, 1545–9.

Jarvis, J. and Lamb, S. (2001) 'Interaction and the development of communication in the under twos: issues for practitioners working with young children in groups', *Early Years* 21, 2, 129–37.

Jenner, S. (1988) 'The influence of additional information, advice and support on the success of breast feeding in working class primiparas', *Child Care Health and Development* 14, 319–28.

Juan-Garau, M. and Perez-Vidal, C. (2001) 'Mixing and pragmatic parental strategies in early bilingual acquisition', *Journal of Child Language* 28: 59–86.

Kellogg, R. (1969) *Analysing Children's Art*. California: National Press Books.

Kenner, C. (2000) *Home Pages Literacy Links for Bilingual Children*. Stoke-on-Trent: Trentham Books.

Ladd, P. (1991) 'Making plans for Nigel: the erosion of identity by mainstreaming', in Taylor, G. and Bishop, J. (eds) *Being Deaf: The Experience of Deafness*. London: Open University.

Laminack, L.L. (1991) *Learning with Zachary*. Richmond Hill, ON: Ashton Scholastic.

Leather, S. (1996) *The Making of Modern Malnutrition: An Overview of Food Poverty in the UK*. London: The Caroline Walker Trust.

Lowenfeld, V. and Brittain, W. L. (1970) *Creative and Mental Growth*. New York: Macmillan.

Lynas, W., Lewis, S. and Hopwood, V. (1997) 'Supporting the education of deaf children in mainstream schools', *Deafness and Education* 21, 2, 41–5.

Malaguzzi, L. (1993) 'History ideas and basic philosophy', in Edwards, C. *et al.* (eds) *The Hundred Languages of Children: The Reggio Amelia Approach to Early Childhood Education*. Norwood, NJ: Ablex.

Malaguzzi, L. (1996) in Edwards, C. *The Hundred Languages of Children: The Reggio Emilia Approach to Early Childhood Education*. Reggio Emilia: Reggio Children s.r.l.

Mallett, R. (1997) 'A parental perspective on partnership' in Wolfendale, S. (ed.) *Working with Parents of SEN Children After the Code of Practice*. London: David Fulton Publishers, pp. 27–40.

Marcschark, M. (1993) *Psychological Development of Deaf Children*. Oxford: Oxford University Press.

Marcschark, M. (2000) 'Education and development of deaf children – or is it development and education?', in Spencer, P., Erting, C. and Marcschark, M. (eds) *The Deaf Child in the Family and at School*. Mahwah, NJ: Lawrence Erlbaum Associates.

Marsh, A. and McKay, S. (1994) *Poor Smokers*. London: Policy Studies Institute.

Marx, J. (1997) 'Iron deficiency in developed countries: prevalence, influence of lifestyle factors and hazards of prevention', *European Journal of Clinical Nutrition* 51, 491–4.

Matthews, J. (1994) *Helping Children to Draw and Paint in Early Childhood: Children and Visual Representation*. London: Hodder and Stoughton.

McGuinness, C. (1999) *From Thinking Skills to Thinking Classrooms: A Review and Evaluation of Approaches for Developing Pupils' Thinking*. Research Report No. 115. Norwich: Her Majesty's Stationery Office.

McLachlan-Smith, C.J. and St. George A.M. (2000) 'Children learn by doing: teachers' beliefs about learning, teaching and literacy in New Zealand kindergartens', *New Zealand Journal of Educational Studies* 35 (1), 37–49.

Meek, M. (1990) 'What do we know about reading that helps us to teach?', in Carter, R. (ed.) *Knowledge about Language and the Curriculum*. London: Hodder and Stoughton.

Mercer, N. (1995) *The Guided Construction of Knowledge Talk among Teachers and Learners*. Clevedon: Multilingual Matters.

Miller, L. (1996) *Toward Reading: Literacy Development in the Pre-School Years*. Buckingham: Open University Press.

Miller, L. (1999) *Moving Towards Literacy with Environmental Print*. Royston, Herts: United Kingdom Reading Association.

Miller, L. (2000) 'Play as a foundation for learning', in Drury, R., Miller, L. and Campbell, R. (eds) *Looking at Early Years Education and Care*. London: David Fulton.

Miller, L., Soler, J. and Woodhead, M. (2002) 'Shaping early childhood education', in Maybin, J. and Woodhead, M. (eds) *Childhoods in Context*. Chichester: John Wiley.

Mills, C. and Mills, D. (1998) *Dispatches: The Early Years*. London: Channel 4 Television.

Ministry of Education (1996) *Te Whaariki Early Childhood Curriculum*. Wellington: Learning Media Ltd.

Ministry of Education (1997–1998) *School Entry Assessment: The First National Picture July 1997–May 1998*. Wellington: Ministry of Education.

Ministry of Education (1998) *Quality in Action Te Mahi Whai Hua*. Wellington: Learning Media Ltd.

Ministry of Education (1999a) *Report of the Literacy Taskforce*. Wellington: Ministry of Education.

Ministry of Education (1999b) *Literacy Experts Group: Report to the Ministry of Education*. Wellington: Ministry of Education.

Minns, H. (1997) *Read it to Me Now: Learning at Home and at School*. Buckingham: Open University Press.

Mittler, P. and Mittler, H. (1982) *Partnership with Parents*. Stratford-upon-Avon: National Council for Special Education.

Monkman, C. (1995) 'Deaf Children in Mainstream Nursery: An Evaluation of the Accessibility of Two Nursery Settings', unpublished MA dissertation, University of Hertfordshire

Moriarty, V. and Siraj-Blatchford, I. (1998) 'Early childhood educators' perceptions of the U.K. Desirable Outcomes for Children's Learning: a research study on the policy implications', *International Journal of Early Childhood*, 30 (1) 56–64.

Mroz, M., Smith, F. and Hardman, F. (2000) 'The discourse of the literacy hour', *Cambridge Journal of Education* 30 (3), 379–90.

Mullender, A. and Morley, R. (1994) *Children Living with Domestic Violence: Putting Men's Abuse of Women on the Child Care Agenda*. London: Whiting and Birch.

Murray, L. and Cooper, P. (eds) (1997) *Postpartum Depression and Child Development*. New York: Guilford Press.

Musselman, C., Mootilal, A. and MacKay, S. (1996) 'The social adjustment of deaf adolescents in segregated, partially integrated and mainstream settings', *Journal of Deaf Studies and Deaf Education* 1 (1), 52–63.

Nichol, J. (1999) 'Murder! Literacy and history', *Reading* 33 (2), 78–86.

Northern Ireland Council for the Curriculum, Examinations and Assessment (1997) *Curricular Guidance for Pre-School Education.* Northern Ireland: Council for the Curriculum, Examinations and Assessment.

Nsamenang, A.B. and Lamb, M.E. (1993) 'The acquisition of socio-cognition competence by NSO children in Bamenda grassfields of Northwest Cameroon', *International Journal of Behavioural Development* **16** (3), 429–41.

Nunes, T., Pretzlik, U. and Olsson, J. (2001) 'Deaf children's social relationships in mainstream schools', *Deafness and Education International* **3** (3) 123–36.

Office of Population Censuses and Surveys (1994) *Child Accident Statistics 1993.* London: HMSO.

Office of Population Censuses and Surveys (1995) *The Health of Our Children: Decennial Supplement.* Series DS no. 11. London: HMSO.

Paige-Smith, A. (1996) 'Choosing to campaign: a case study of parent choice, statementing and integration', *European Journal of Special Needs Education* **11**, (3), 321–9.

Parke, T.H. (1993) 'When does the language teacher teach language?' Paper given at the British Association for Applied Linguistics Seminar on Bilingual Classroom Discourse, University of Lancaster.

Parke, T.H. and Drury, R. (2000) 'Coming out of their shells: the speech and language of two young bilinguals in the classroom', *International Journal of Early Years Education* **8** (2): 101–12.

Parke, T.H. and Drury, R. (2001) 'Language development at home and school: gains and losses in young bilinguals', *Early Years* **21** (2), 117–27.

Parr, M. (1996) 'Support for couples in the transition to parenthood', unpublished PhD thesis, University of East London.

Payton, S. (1984) 'Developing awareness of print: a young child's first steps towards literacy', *Educational Review,* University of Birmingham.

Petterson, S. and Burke Albers, A. (2001) 'Effects of poverty and maternal depression on early child development', *Child Development* **72** (6) 1794–813.

Piaget, J. (1951) *Play, Dreams and Imitation in Childhood.* London: Routledge and Kegan Paul.

Piaget, J. (1959) *The Language and Thought of the Child.* 3rd edn. London: Routledge.

Plaskow, D. (ed.) *The Crucial Years.* London: Society for Education through Art.

Pound, L. (1999) *Supporting Mathematical Development in the Early Years.* Buckingham: Open University Press.

Powers, S., Gregory, S. and Thoutenhoofd, E.D. (1998) *The Educational Achievements of Deaf Children.* London: DfEE.

Punch, S. (2001) 'Household division of labour: generation, gender, birth order and sibling composition', *Work, Employment and Society* **15** (4), 803–23.

Qualifications and Curriculum Authority (2000) *Curriculum Guidance for the Foundation Stage.* London: Qualifications and Curriculum Authority.

Qualifications and Curriculum Authority (1999a) *Early Years Education, Childcare and Playwork: A Framework of Nationally Accredited Qualifications.* London: Qualifications and Curriculum Authority.

Qualifications and Curriculum Authority (1999b) *Early Learning Goals.* London: Qualifications and Curriculum Authority.

Qualifications and Curriculum and Assessment Authority for Wales (2000) *Desirable Outcomes for Children's Learning before Compulsory School Age.* Wales: QCAAW.

Qvortrop, J. (1998) 'Childhood exclusion by default', unpublished paper presented at Children and Social Exclusion Conference, University of Hull.

Qvortrop, J. (2001) 'School work, paid work and the changing obligations of children', in Mizen, P., Pole, C. and Bolton, A. (eds) *Hidden Hands: International Perspectives on Children's Work and Labour.* London: Routledge/Falmer.

Ratey, J. (2001) *A User's Guide to the Brain.* London: Little, Brown & Co.

Rath, L.E. (1986) *Teaching for Thinking.* New York: Teachers College Press.

Rheingold, H. (1982) 'Little children's participation in the work of adults, a nascent pro-social behavior', *Child Development* **53**, 114–25.

Rieser, R. (2001) 'New Act a turning point, disability, Special Educational Needs and the law', *Inclusion Now* **2**, 4–5.

Riley, J. (1996a) 'The ability to label the letters of the alphabet at school entry: a discussion on its value', *Journal of Research in Reading* **19** (2), 87–101.

Riley, J. (1996b) *The Teaching of Reading: The Development of Literacy in the Early Years.* London: Paul Chapman.

Rinaldi, C. (1995) 'The emergent curriculum and social constructivism: an interview with Lella Gandini', in Edwards, C., Gandini, L. and Forman, G. (eds) *The Hundred Languages of Children: The Reggio Emilia Approach to Early Childhood Education.* Norwood, NJ: Ablex Publishing Corporation.

Roberts, H. (2000) *What Works in Reducing Inequalities in Child Health?* London: Barnardo's.

Roden, J. (1999) 'Young children are natural scientists', in David, T. (ed.) *Young Children Learning.* London: Paul Chapman Publishing, pp. 130–55.

Rodgers, R. (1999) *Planning an Appropriate Curriculum for the Under Fives.* London: David Fulton.

Rogoff, B. (1990) *Apprenticeship in Thinking: Cognitive Development in Social Context.* New York: Oxford University Press.

Rogoff, B., Mistry, J., Göncü, A. and Mosier, C. (1993) 'Guided Participation in Cultural Activity by Toddlers and Caregivers'. Monograph of the Society for Research in Child Development **58** (8), No. 236.

Royal National Institute for Deaf People (2001) *Education Guidelines Project: Effective Early Intervention for Deaf Children 0–5 and their Families.* London: RNID.

SCAA (1997) *Baseline Assessment Scales.* London: School Curriculum and Assessment Authority.

Schickedanz, J.A. (1990) *Adam's Righting Revolutions.* Portsmouth, NH: Heinemann.

School Curriculum and Assessment Authority (1996) *Desirable Outcomes for Children's Learning on Entering Compulsory Education.* London: Department for Education and Employment/School Curriculum and Assessment Authority.

Schwab, J. (1978) 'Education and the structure of the disciplines', in Westbury, I. and Wilkof, N.J. (eds) *Science, Curriculum and Liberal Education.* Chicago: University of Chicago Press, pp. 229–72.

Schwab, J.J. (1964) 'The structure of the disciplines: meanings and significances', in

Ford, G. and Purgo, L. (eds) *The Structure of Knowledge and the Curriculum.* Chicago: Rand McNally.

Scottish Consultative Council on the Curriculum (1999) *Curriculum Framework for Children 3 to 5.* Scotland: Scottish Consultative Council on the Curriculum.

Select Committee on Education and Employment (2000) *First Report: Early Years.*

Selleck, D. (1997) 'Baby art: art is me', in Gura, P. (ed.) *Reflections on Early Education and Care.* London: British Association for Early Childhood Education.

Seuss, Dr (1960) *Green Eggs and Ham.* New York: Random House.

Sheridan, M. (2000) 'Images of self and others: stories from the children', in Spencer, P., Erting, C. and Marcschark, M. (eds) *The Deaf Child in the Family and at School.* Mahwah, NJ: Lawrence Erlbaum Associates.

Singer, E. (1992) *Childcare and the Psychology of Development.* London: Routledge.

Siraj-Blatchford, J. and Macleod-Brudnell, I. (1999) *Supporting Science, Design and Technology in the Early Years.* Buckingham: Open University Press.

Smith, F. (1971) *Understanding Reading.* Toronto: Holt Rinehart & Winston.

Smith, J., Brooks-Gunn, J. and Klebanov, P. (1997) 'The consequences of living in poverty for young children's cognitive and verbal ability and early school achievement', in Duncan, G. and Brooks-Gunn, J. (eds) *Consequences of Growing Up Poor.* New York: Sage, pp. 132–89.

Soler, J. (1999) 'Past and present technocratic solutions to teaching literacy: implications for New Zealand primary teachers and literacy programmes', *Pedagogy, Culture and Society: Journal of Educational Discussion and Debate* 7 (3), 523–40.

Steele, B. (1998) *Draw Me a Story: An Illustrated Exploration of Drawing-as-a-language.* Winnipeg, Canada: Peguis.

Stern, D. (1998) *The Interpersonal World of the Infant.* London: Karnac Books.

Stowe, W. and Haydn. T. (2000) Issues in the teaching of chronology, in Arthur, J. and Phillips R. (eds) *Issues in History Teaching.* London: Routledge, pp. 83–97.

Strickland, D.S. (1998) *Teaching Phonics Today: A Primer for Educators.* Newark, DE: International Reading Association.

Sulzby, E. (1990) 'Assessment of writing and children's language while writing', in Mandel-Morrow, L. and Smith, J.K. (eds) *Assessment for Instruction in Early Literacy.* New Jersey: Prentice-Hall.

Super, C. and Harkness, S. (1986) 'The developmental niche: a conceptualisation at the interface of child and culture', *International Journal of Behavioral Development* 9, 545–69.

Sure Start (2001) *A Guide for Fourth Wave Programmes.* Nottingham: Department for Education and Employment Publications.

Swann, W. (1987) 'Statements of intent: an assessment of reality', in Booth, T. and Swann, W. (eds) *Including Pupils with Disabilities.* Milton Keynes: Open University Press.

Tarone, E. and Liu, G.-Q. (1995) 'Situational context, variation, and second language acquisition theory', in Cook, G. and Seidlhofer, B. (eds) *Principle and Practice in Applied Linguistics.* Oxford: Oxford University Press.

Tate Maltby, M. and Knight, P. (2000) *Audiology: An Introduction for Teachers and Other Professionals.* London: David Fulton.

Teale, W. (1984) 'Reading to young children: its significance for literacy development', in Goelman, H., Oberg, A. and Smith, F. (eds) *Awakening to Literacy*. London: Heinemann.

The Literacy Taskforce (1997) *A Reading Revolution: How Can We Teach Every Child to Read Well?* The Preliminary Report of the Literacy Taskforce, London: Institute of Education.

Thomas, G. (1997) 'Inclusive schools for an inclusive society', *British Journal of Special Education* **24** (3), 103–7.

Thurlbeck, S. (2000) 'Growing up in Britain, Review', *British Medical Journal* **320**, 809.

Tietjen, A.M. (1989) 'The ecology of children's social support networks', in Belle, D. (ed.) *Children's Social Networks and Social Supports*. New York: John Wiley.

Titmuss, R. (1943) *Birth, Poverty and Wealth*. London: Hamish Hamilton.

Tizard, B. and Hughes, M. (1984) *Young Children Learning*. London: Collins.

Trelease, J. (1995) *The New Read-Aloud Handbook*. London: Penguin Books.

Trevelyan, G.M. (1913) 'Clio, a Muse', *Independent Review*. December edition.

TSO (2000) *Race Relations (Amendment) Act*. London: TSO.

Turner-Bisset, R.A. (2000) 'Meaningful history with young children', in Drury, R., Miller, L. and Campbell, R. (eds) *Looking at Early Years Education and Care*. London: David Fulton, pp. 170–8.

Turner-Bisset, R.A. (2001) 'Learning to love history: preparation of non-specialist primary teachers to teach history, *Teaching History* **102**, February, 36–41.

Underdown, A. (1998a) 'Investigating techniques used in parenting classes', *Health Visitor* **71** (2), 65–8.

Underdown, A. (1998b) 'The transition to parenthood', *The British Journal of Midwifery* **6** (8), 508–11.

United Nations (1989) *The Conventions on the Rights of the Child*. New York: UNICEF.

Upton, M., Watt, G., Davy Smith, G. *et al.* (1998) 'Permanent effects of maternal smoking on offsprings' lung function', *Lancet* **352**, 453.

Van der Eyken, W. (1973) *Child, Family and Society*. Harmondsworth: Penguin.

Vygotksy, L.S. (1978) *Mind in Society: The Development of Higher Mental Processes*. Cambridge, MA: Harvard University Press.

Vygotsky, L. (1986) *Thought and Language*. Cambridge, MA: MIT Press.

Wade, B. (ed.) (1990) *Reading for Real*. Buckingham: Open University Press.

Watkins, K. (2000) *The Oxfam Education Report*. Oxford: Oxfam.

Weisner T. S. (1989) 'Cultural and universal aspects of social support for children: evidence from the Abaluyia of Kenya', in Belle, D. (ed.) *Children's Social Networks and Social Supports*. New York: John Wiley.

Wells, G. (1986) *The Meaning Makers: Children Learning Language and Using Language to Learn*. London: Hodder and Stoughton.

Whitehead, M. (1999a) *Supporting Language and Literacy Development in the Early Years*. Buckingham: Open University Press.

Whitehead, M. (1999b) 'A literacy hour in the nursery? The big question mark', *Early Years* **19** (2) 51–61.

Whiting, B.B. and Whiting, J. (1975) *Children of Six Cultures: A Psycho-cultural Analysis*. Cambridge, MA: Harvard University Press.

Willey, C. (2000) 'Working with parents in early years settings', in Drury, R., Miller, L. and Campbell, R. (eds) *Looking at Early Years Education and Care*. London: David Fulton.

Winnicott, D. (1960) 'The theory of parent-infant relationships', *International Journal of Psychoanalysis* **41**, 585–95.

Wolfendale, S. (2000) 'Special needs in the early years; prospects for policy and practice', *Support for Learning* **15** (4), 147–51.

Wood, D., Wood, H., Griffiths, A. and Howarth, I. (1986) *Teaching and Talking with Deaf Children*. Chichester: John Wiley.

Wood, E. and Holden, C. (1995) *Teaching Early Years History*. Cambridge: Chris Kington Publishing.

Wood, S. (1995) 'Developing an understanding of time-sequencing issues', *Teaching History* **79**, April, 11–14.

Woodhead, J. (2001) 'Using attachment theory and the concepts of holding and containment in group work with parents and infants, from birth to three years', unpublished conference paper, Pen Green. March, Corby.

Woodhead, M. (1989) 'School starts at five . . . or four years old? The rationale for changing admission policies in England and Wales', *Journal of Education Policy* **4** (1), 1–21.

Woodhead, M. (1996) *In Search of the Rainbow: Pathways to Quality in Large Scale Programmes for Young Disadvantaged Children*. The Hague: Bernard van Leer Foundation.

Woodhead, M. (1998) *Children's perspectives on their working lives*. Stockholm: Radda Barnen (Save the Children Sweden).

Woodhead, M. (1999a) 'Combating child labour: listen to what the children say', *Childhood* **6** (1), 27–49.

Woodhead, M. (1999b) 'Reconstructing developmental psychology: some first steps', *Children and Society* **13** (1), 3–19.

Woods, D. (1998) *How Children Think and Learn,* 2nd edn. Oxford: Blackwell.

Wylie, C., Thompson, J. and Hendricks A. K. (1996) *Competent Children at 5: Families and Early Education*. Wellington: New Zealand Council for Educational Research.

Zelizer, V.A. (1985) *Pricing the Priceless Child: The Changing Social Value of Children*. New York: Basic Books.

Index

accidents 114–15
ages, starting 124–6, 127–8
alphabet, knowledge of 19–20, 23–7
attendance 126–7

bilingualism 5
  adult–child relationships and 88–9
  home backgrounds 79–80
  narrow-mindedness towards 78–9
  nursery education and 80–8

child-centred practices
  adult–child relationships and 59–61
  in literacy 9, 13–16, 17–18
  scope 43
curriculum *see individual entries*
Climbie, Victoria 117

deafness, children's 6
  aids for 102, 109–10
  concepts understood by, diverse
    acquisition 103–4
  inclusion for
    from books 109
    challenges 104–5
    from communication 105–6, 107
    from group activities 108
    home backgrounds 105
    from language 107–8
    from listening 106
    from own strengths 109
    from sense of place 106
  language and, diverse acquisition 102–4
  in nursery education 101, 103, 110,
    111
  overhearing and, limitations 103, 104, 108

scope 102–3
degrees 6–7
developmental niche 130–1
diet 114, 115
  schemes 117–18
diversity, children's 5
  specific *see individual entries*
domestic violence 116
double-blind trials 69
drawing, as language 4
  adult–child relationships and 48, 49–51
  analysed 42–3
  common features 42
  developing 45–7, 49
  narratives from 43–4, 50
  preliminary 40–1, 43
  recording 48
  scope 40–2, 43, 44–5, 50–1

Early Childhood Literacy Project 16–18
equality 4
  specific *see individual entries*
ethics, in research 72–3
experiment 67, 68
exploration 3, 4
  in literacy 14

formal practices 2–3
  in literacy 9–10, 12–13, 17

gender 128
groups
  for deafness, children's 108
  Growing Together 120–1
  for parents of SEN children 94–8
guided participation 132–3

Hawthorne effect 69
health and safety, children's 6
  attainment and 116
  emerging threats 113–17
  good health 112
  mental health issues 113
    depression 115
  partnerships in 118–21, 122
  policy-making on 112–13, 116–22
  social factors 112
    domestic violence 116
    parents' smoking 115
    poverty 113–17
history 4
  adult–child relationships and 33
  character-based 36–9
  concepts understood in 32, 33, 36
  evidence in 29–30, 37–9
  literacy and 37–9
  map for planning 30, 31, 36
  representation and 28, 30, 32–3, 35
  scope 36
  time understood in, limitations 28–9, 33,
    34–6
Home Zones 118
homes
  bilingualism and 78–9
  deafness, children's and 105

inclusion 4–6, 93, 110–11
  specific see individual entries
internet, research from 66–7

language
  adult-generated 86, 87
  aims in 86–7, 88
  bilingualism see bilingualism
  child-generated 86–7
  deafness, children's and
    diverse acquisition 102–4
    inclusion 107–8
  drawing as see drawing, as language
  scope 3, 50
  sign language 102–3, 107
literacy 3–4
  adult–child relationships and 8–9, 26–7
    limitations 12, 24–5
  alphabet, knowledge and 19–20, 23–7
  child-centred practices and 9, 13–16,
    17–18
  consultation in 13–14
  exploration in 14

formal practices and 9–10, 12–13, 17
  goals in 11–12, 19–20
  history and 37–9
  materials for 20–1, 25, 26
  narrative in 21–3
  patterns and 21, 22
  play in 13, 17, 20–1
  preconceptions in 9, 10–11, 15
  preliminary signs 19
  print and 23
  project 16–18
  representation and 20, 21, 22–3
  scope 25, 26–7
  shared reading and 22, 23, 26
  talk and 20
  writing name correctly and 19–20, 23–7

mathematics
  adult–child relationships in 54–7
  concepts understood in 58–9
  curiosity in 4, 54–6
  initiative in 59
  materials for 58
  play in, recording 54–7, 58
  questions in 55–7, 60–1
  reasoning in 55–6, 57
mimicry 40, 129–30
motor development 131

narratives 21–3
  from drawing 43–4, 50
  time understood in, limitations 28–9, 33,
    34–6
National School Fruit Scheme 117
nursery education
  bilingualism and
    adult-generated language 86
    diverse acquisition 82–3, 87–8
    early progress 80–1
    errors 82–4, 88
    imperatives used 84, 85
    observation 81–8
    scope 85–6
    shared acquisition 84
  deafness, children's and 101, 103, 110,
    111

observation 54–7, 58, 68, 81–8

parents
  of SEN children 5–6
    coping mechanisms 92

groups for 94–8
narrow-mindedness towards 91, 92–3, 96–8
partnerships in 90, 91, 98–9, 119–21, 122
policy-making on 90–1, 98–100
smoking by 115
on work by children 127, 129–30, 131–2, 133–4
placebos 69
planning 2
map for, in history 30, 31, 36
play 5, 52, 124, 125
cultural factors 130, 131
in literacy 13, 17, 20–1
materials for 58
in mathematics, recording 54–7, 58
principle factors 130
social factors 130
policy-making 5
on health and safety 112–13, 116–22
on SEN children 90–1, 98–100
on work by children 124–6
poverty
accidents and 115
diet and 114, 115
as emerging threat 113–14
social factors
domestic violence 116
parents' smoking 115

qualifications 6–7
questions
in mathematics 55–7, 60–1
in research 65–7, 73
in science 53, 54, 60–1

reading see literacy
research 4
adult–child relationships and 63
on bilingualism 79–88
on child-centred practices 41–2
on drawing, as preliminary language 43
ethics in 72–3
experiment in 67, 68
groundwork in 67
history project 33–5
from internet 66–7

literacy project 16–18
measurement in 71–2
observation in 68
preconceptions, countering 62, 69–70, 74
qualitative 63, 64–5, 66–73
quantitative 63–5, 66–73
questions in 65–7, 73
sample specificity 70–1
scope 62–3
selection in 65
safety see health and safety, children's
science
adult–child relationships and 53–4
concepts understood in 58–9
curiosity in 4, 52, 53–4, 56
initiative in 59
materials for 58
questions in 53, 54, 60–1
reasoning in 54, 56, 57
SEN (special educational needs) children
coping mechanisms with 92
deafness see deafness, children's
inclusion, limitations 94–8, 101–2
narrow-mindedness towards 91, 92–3, 96–8
policy-making on 90–1, 98–100
stories see narratives
Sure Start 119–21, 122

time see history
training 6–7
Warnock Report 91
work, children's 6
adult–child relationships and 132–3
attendance and 126–7
as contribution 129–30
cultural factors 130, 131–3
economic work
cultural factors 127–9
gender factors 128
scope 124–6, 127–8
parents on 127, 129–30, 131–2, 133–4
policy-making on 124–6
principle factors 130
scope 133–4
social factors 130
writing see literacy